THE AMERICAN REVOLUTION

D0725978

PROBLEMS IN AMERICAN HISTORY

EDITOR

LOREN BARITZ

State University of New York, Albany

THE AMERICAN REVOLUTION

The Search For Meaning

EDITED BY

RICHARD J. HOOKER

JOHN WILEY & SONS, INC.

NEW YORK · LONDON · SYDNEY · TORONTO

Copyright © 1970, by John Wiley & Sons, Inc.

All rights reserved. No part of this book may be reproduced
by any means, nor transmitted, nor translated into a machine
language without the written permission of the publisher.

10 9 8 7 6 5 4 3

Library of Congress Catalogue Card Number: 76-199321

Cloth: SBN 471 40890 5   Paper: SBN 471 40891 3

Printed in the United States of America

SERIES PREFACE

This series is an introduction to the most important problems in the writing and study of American history. Some of these problems have been the subject of debate and argument for a long time, although others only recently have been recognized as controversial. However, in every case, the student will find a vital topic, an understanding of which will deepen his knowledge of social change in America.

The scholars who introduce and edit the books in this series are teaching historians who have written history in the same general area as their individual books. Many of them are leading scholars in their fields, and all have done important work in the collective search for better historical understanding.

Because of the talent and the specialized knowledge of the individual editors, a rigid editorial format has not been imposed on them. For example, some of the editors believe that primary source material is necessary to their subjects. Some believe that their material should be arranged to show conflicting interpretations. Others have decided to use the selected materials as evidence for their own interpretations. The individual editors have been given the freedom to handle their books in the way that their own experience and knowledge indicate is best. The overall result is a series built up from the individual decisions of working scholars in the various fields, rather than one that conforms to a uniform editorial decision.

A common goal (rather than a shared technique) is the bridge of this series. There is always the desire to bring the reader as close to these problems as possible. One result of this objective is an emphasis of the nature and consequences of problems and events, with a de-emphasis of the more purely historiographical issues. The goal is to involve the student in the reality of crisis, the inevitability of ambiguity, and the excitement of finding a way through the historical maze.

Above all, this series is designed to show students how experienced historians read and reason. Although health is not contagious, intellectual engagement may be. If we show students something significant in a phrase or a passage that they otherwise may have missed, we will have accomplished part of our objective. When students see something that passed us by, then the process will have been made whole. This active and mutual involvement of editor and reader with a significant human problem will rescue the study of history from the smell and feel of dust.

Loren Baritz

CONTENTS

vii

THE AMERICAN REVOLUTION

INTRODUCTION

The search for the meaning of the American Revolution began during the Revolution, has continued ever since, and will continue as long as men find the subject important and interesting. There has never been complete agreement on the subject in the past nor is there likely to be in the future. Although scholars have occasionally implied that their researches have laid bare *the* truth and that earlier interpretations could be discarded, no one has yet altered the fact that each generation writes its own history, injecting into the past some of the convictions, biases, and interests that are influential at a given time.

The historians of the American Revolution have turned in thought and research to a number of basic questions, each of which has received a variety of answers. Some questions relate to the scope of the Revolution in time and space. Are its sources to be traced back to the first settlements or were they largely confined to the fifteen years preceding the outbreak of the war? Or, as Benjamin Rush once said, was the Revolution only in its early stages in 1787? If continuity in American history is as pronounced as some recent historians have suggested, is the American Revolution perhaps still continuing, its basic principles still unfolding? Closely related are questions of the consequences of the American Revolution. Did they end with the framing of the Constitution, with the victory of Jacksonian democracy, or are they appearing in the civil rights struggles of the present century? What of the impact of the American Revolution on eighteenth-century Europe, on Latin-America, and, as some believe, even on the Asian and African revolutions of the twentieth century?

Equally difficult to answer are questions of the nature of the American Revolution. Should one study the Revolution as an

1

aspect of British imperial history or should it be approached as a national movement? Was the Revolution simply a war for independence or did it also involve a struggle of classes within the colonies for social, economic, and political power? Did the revolutionary movement have broad popular support or did a relatively few interested leaders inveigle the great mass of the people into the contest? To what extent were the recurrent crises after 1763 that culminated in war due to the stupidity, error, or even wickedness of George III, the ministry, or Parliament? Were ideas important in themselves during the revolutionary movement or were they rather rationalizations of the colonial position, to be modified as circumstances required? Were the changes that occurred in American society during and after the American Revolution the results of that movement or were they rather the extensions of long-developing trends or the by-products of quite different causes?

Differences of interpretation were never so sharp as during the Revolutionary era itself. The historians—whether patriot or loyalist—included some of the better minds in the emerging nation. Among the patriot historians were the Reverend William Gordon and Mercy Otis Warren, both of Massachusetts, and Dr. David Ramsay of South Carolina; the loyalist writers included Thomas Hutchinson and Peter Oliver, both of Massachusetts, Thomas Jones of New York, Joseph Galloway of Pennsylvania, and George Chalmers of Maryland.

Many of these amateur historians—Ramsay, Hutchinson, Oliver, Jones, and Galloway—had held positions of influence and some of considerable power and all had had access to influential circles. All, but most particularly the loyalists who had suffered defeat, revealed in their writings the marks of exposure to war and revolution. If their weaknesses are the sometimes violent biases that result from this experience of conflict, their strength appears in the knowledge, the observations, and the insights that can come only from first-hand participation in a moment of history. Both groups tried to interpret the motives of the leading revolutionary figures and often cast these leaders in heroic or diabolic molds. Although they disagreed considerably on the nature of the revolutionary movement, Merrill Jensen has pointed out that both patriot and loyalist historians generally agreed that a relatively

few leaders had exerted an immense influence, that the idea of
independence had appeared early, and that the great mass of the
people had been quite indifferent to the idea.[1]

A new interpretation of the Revolution was offered by George
Bancroft during the strident, enthusiastic nationalism of the Jacksonian era. His well-researched *History of the United States* was
to dominate the thought of successive generations until the end
of the century and beyond.

Bancroft, scholarly and cultured, began his task in the 1830's
and expended large amounts of money and effort in the collection
of sources. He did not publish his last two volumes, in a total of
twelve, until 1882. This great history, about two-thirds of which
was concerned with the American Revolution, was dominated by
certain over-riding convictions. The author's patriotism and
religious faith intermingled: the intent of God appeared in all
history. Under divine guidance the world was moving in the
direction of human liberty. American independence was a presage
of the future and the patriots were but agents of God's will.

More mundanely, Bancroft, an advocate of low tariffs, found
that British mercantilism had been an important cause of colonial
anger and revolution, an interpretation that was to be generally
accepted until quite recently. He also pictured a wicked George
III who had led Great Britain in a war against human rights, an
image that was also long to endure.

The intense nationalism in Bancroft's interpretation won him
approval for two-thirds of a century, whereas his highly dramatic
style and his interest in colorful detail made his *History* readable
and popular. And if his subject matter was overwhelmingly
political, military, and occasionally religious, in this too he did
not affront his times.

By the late nineteenth century new currents of thought and
feeling began to make Bancroft appear old-fashioned and un-
acceptable. The country entered a period of agrarian protests,
of fear of big business, and of recognition of social ills. Historians,
like politicians, became more aware of social and economic forces.

---

[1] Merrill Jensen, "Historians and the Nature of the American Revolution,"
in *The Reinterpretation of Early American History: Essays in Honor of John
Edwin Pomfret*, Ray Allen Billington, ed. San Marino, Calif., 1966, pp. 113–14.

From Europe came the ideas of Marx. In American universities a growing number of scholars appeared, often trained in German seminars, in the fields of sociology, political science, economics, and history. Their work inevitably prepared the way for history written with a wider scope than had seemed necessary before.

This socio-economic school of historians represented a radical change from Bancroft. Such scholars as Charles H. Lincoln, Carl Becker, Arthur M. Schlesinger, J. Franklin Jameson, Charles A. Beard, Vernon L. Parrington, and later Merrill Jensen vastly increased the scope and complexity of American Revolutionary studies by giving great emphasis to social and economic influences, by often audacious attempts to explain historical motivation, and by the use of categories of source material that had hitherto been neglected. In contrast to the heavily political and constitutional approach of Bancroft, Americans were now given a treatment of the Revolution which, less in the heroic tradition and much more complicated, involved class, sectional, and economic divisions that sometimes accentuated and sometimes conflicted with the concurrent struggles of colonists against British power.

These revisionist historians paid considerable attention to the fifteen years that preceded the War of Independence. Their interest in social and economic change and conflict led them to focus also on the consequences of the Revolution, on the period of the Articles of Confederation, and on the "counter-revolution" that some of them saw in the Constitutional Convention.

In general, this new group of historians described a colonial order in which eastern planters and merchants were politically, economically, and socially dominant. When, after the French and Indian War, the British government imposed new taxes and regulations on the colonies, this leading class led the opposition and won over the lower classes as allies. The lower-class leaders, however, soon began to agitate for a more equalitarian order and made demands that the ruling class found dangerous to its own interests. The American Revolution, then, became a dual movement with an "external" aspect which had independence of England as its goal and an "internal" contest between the upper and lower orders of society for ascendancy. This struggle continued after the war. The Articles of Confederation reflected the wishes of the more democratic interests, but after six years the upper classes negotiated a virtual counter-revolution by drafting a Constitution that was intended to protect their interests and to suppress the dangers of "excessive" democracy.

Historians of this new school sometimes stated, or implied, that the constitutional arguments of colonial patriots were not to be taken literally but were rather to be understood as cloaking economic or social interests. Scholarship served as an academic X-ray by which the solid structure of real motives was revealed beneath the outer sheath of words. Ideas were effective—as the studies of propaganda by Philip Davidson and Arthur M. Schlesinger showed—but they were not to be understood too literally. It was a viewpoint that hardly encouraged studies of the intellectual background of the Revolution.

Another important approach to the colonial period, with implications for the Revolutionary era, appeared about the turn of the century. During the late nineteenth century the United States became increasingly aware of the foreign scene, whereas Great Britain, faced by the growing military power of Germany, began to promote friendly relations with the United States. As a byproduct of these changes, American historians, like the public at large, began to think less harshly of the behavior of the English during the Revolution and even to regard the loyalists with greater tolerance. As closer ties with Great Britain developed, later aided by Anglo-American alliances in two world wars, so also grew a desire for historical treatments of the American Revolution that were less provincial than that of Bancroft. The result was a group of historians who in time were named the "imperial" school. Led by George Louis Beer, Herbert L. Osgood, Charles M. Andrews, and Lawrence H. Gipson, these men compiled an impressive array of works on the colonial period. They plucked early American history from its nationalistic context and tried to examine it as an aspect of British imperial history. In place of provincialism, critics claimed, they substituted at times a pro-British bias.

In general, the imperial historians found that the British Empire had been well administered. The King, ministry, and Parliament had not been to blame for the break with the colonies.

Rather, the American Revolution had resulted from an evolutionary development in which the distinctive physical environment of the American colonies produced a unique political and social order. This new American society found it increasingly difficult to communicate with a British government that reflected the attitudes of a quite different society. The basic causes of the Revolution, then, were conflicts in ideology and outlook, which in turn were the result of a century and a half of divergent growth.

The decline of Anglophobia, together with the work of the imperialist historians, provided a sympathetic background for new studies of the long-neglected loyalists, a subject almost completely ignored by the patriot historians and Bancroft. Various studies of state and regional loyalism were followed in 1902 by a general study by Claude Van Tyne. More recently research of greater depth has been undertaken by William R. Nelson and others.

During the late 1920's the Whig interpretation of Bancroft came under attack from still another source. Sir Lewis Namier in 1929 published the first of a series of detailed examinations of late eighteenth-century English politics to be done by him and his disciples, including Eric Robson in the United States. These Namierists pictured George III not as a tyrant but rather as a monarch who had acted within his political rights. Nor had the years before the War of Independence seen a real confrontation by Whig and Tory parties in England, for instead of parties the Namierist historians discovered only factions which were under the influence of family and local interests and quite unable to act in a consistent or statesmanlike manner. Clearly there was room for conflict between the Namierists, who held that the British government was incapable of a consistently good administration, and the imperialist historians who maintained that the empire had been generally well administered.

The search for the meaning of the American Revolution took still another turn after World War II. A spreading affluence promoted middle-class complacency and a tendency to minimize economic and social grievances. And in a world in which sharp and sometimes violent changes were becoming commonplace in every field of human activity from science to politics the American Revolution began to appear less revolutionary—indeed, to some, not revolutionary at all. A new group of historians appeared who were to be labeled neo-Whig, conservatives, or nationalists and included as key figures Edmund S. Morgan, Daniel Boorstin, Louis Hartz, Robert E. Brown, Clinton Rossiter, Forrest McDonald, Cecelia Kenyon, and Bernard Bailyn. Although there were great differences of interpretation among them, scholars of this new school would have largely agreed to an account of the Revolution that was in sharp conflict with that of either imperialist or socio-economic historians.

The American colonies before 1760 were seen as generally content with British rule. The colonists had a high degree of prosperity and self-government with an extensive franchise and powerful representative assemblies. The Navigation Acts, too, were largely benign in their influence, but about 1760 the picture changed. The new colonial policy of Great Britain encompassed a whole series of attacks on American rights and liberties. In defense of these rights American leaders acted as conservatives in defending the status quo but as liberals in that they protected human rights against a self-seeking and conservative British regime.

The neo-Whig historians found little conflict in the colonies over social and economic issues. Unlike the socio-economic historians, therefore, they did not see the constitutional arguments of the patriotic leaders as a camouflage to hide such issues. Rather, the constitutional writings expressed American principles that were consistently maintained during the entire Revolutionary period. Indeed, the neo-Whigs made much of the continuity in American history.

Since these historians found no class struggle in the revolutionary movement, so too they found no important enlargement of democracy. The Articles of Confederation, therefore, could hardly be considered a consolidation of democratic gains nor could the Constitution be thought of as an upper-class counter-revolution. In short, during the entire period from 1760 to 1787 there had not really been an American Revolution in the sense of a basic shift in the source of political power or a major reconstruction of American society. Any movement toward greater democracy that had occurred was but a continuation of long-existing trends.

The similarity between the neo-Whigs and Bancroft has often

been pointed out. In many ways it exists: the emphasis on political and constitutional issues, the conviction that the American cause was just, the concentration on the issues of the fifteen years before the war, the idea that independence was the central goal with the Constitution as its culmination all evoke Bancroft. There are, however, important differences: a less strident nationalism and none of the piety, a greater awareness of the complexities of historical causation, a more profound analysis of events, a lively sense of intellectual factors, and the benefit of the research of innumerable scholars since Bancroft.

Criticism of, and self-criticism by, the neo-Whigs has been voiced. It has been charged, for instance, that they have made the Revolution too polite and sedate an affair, whereas in fact it involved great turmoil and social dislocations. Again, it is said that the neglect of the loyalists has overemphasized both the consensus and the continuity of the Revolutionary era. And, of course, there have been sharp denials that the colonial population was lacking in feudal-like divisions of rich and poor, weak and strong, or that there had been no major gains in political democracy.

Other interpretations of the Revolution will be forthcoming and only partly because of newly discovered sources and fresh scholarship. More important will be the appearance of novel situations that will suggest, or demand, different understandings of the past. Even today the work of some historians shows the influence of the civil rights struggles and the New Left in politics. In the future, as in the past, "the truth" about the American Revolution will appear whenever a given generation finds itself satisfied with its chosen meaning of that phase of history.

1

John Adams
"But what do we mean by the American Revolution?"

Aware of the infinite complexity of history, the inadequacy of extant sources, and the unwillingness of later generations to hear hard truths about heroic forbears, John Adams never attempted to write a formal history of the American Revolution. Yet he thought often about the subject, and on various occasions he outlined to correspondents the events that had led to the Revolution and the consequent War of Independence.

The following letter was addressed to Hezekiah Niles, editor of the Weekly Register. Niles was a strong nationalist who had displayed a genuine interest in American history. Adams, eighty-two years old, offered a later generation the wise guidance of one who had lived through and understood a great moment of American history.

The American Revolution was not a common Event. Its Effects and Consequences have already been Awful over a great Part of the Globe. And when and where are they to cease?

But what do we mean by the American Revolution? Do we mean the American War? The Revolution was effected before the War commenced. The Revolution was in the Minds and Hearts of the People. A Change in their Religious Sentiments of their Duties and Obligations. While the King, and all in Author-

SOURCE. John Adams to Hezekiah Niles, Quincy, Mass., February 13, 1818. Manuscript letter in the collections of the Maryland Historical Society.

ity under him, were believed to govern, in Justice and Mercy according to the Laws and Constitutions derived to them from the God of Nature, and tra[n]smitted to them by their Ancestors, they thought themselves bound to pray for the King and Queen and all the Royal Family, and all in Authority under them, as Ministers ordained of God for their good. But when they saw those Powers renouncing all the Principles of Authority, and bent upon the destruction of all the Securities of their Lives, Liberties and Properties, they thought it their Duty to pray for the Continental Congress and all the thirteen State Congresses, &c.

There might be, and there were others, who thought less about Religion and Conscience, but had certain habitual Sentiments of Allegiance and Loyalty derived from their Education; but believing Allegiance and Protection to be reciprocal, when Protection was withdrawn, they thought Allegiance was dissolved.

Another Alteration was common to all. The People of America had been educated in an habitual Affection for England as their Mother-Country; and while they thought her a kind and tender Parent, (erroneously enough, however, for she never was such a Mother,) no Affection could be more Sincere. But when they found her a cruel Beldam, willing, like Lady Macbeth, to dash their Brains out, it is no Wonder if their fillial Affections ceased and were changed into Indignation and horror.

This radi[c]al Change in the Principles, Opinions Sentiments and Affections of the People, was the real American Revolution.

By what means, this great and important Alteration in the religious, moral, political and social Character of the People of thirteen Colonies, all distinct, unconnected and independent of each other, was begun, pursued and accomplished, it is surely interesting to Humanity to investigate, and perpetuate to Posterity.

To this End it is greatly to be desired that Young Gentlemen of Letters in all the States, especially in the thirteen original States, would undertake the laborious, but certainly interesting and amusing Task, of Searching and collecting all the Records, Pamphlets, Newspapers and even hand-Bills, which in any Way contributed to change the Temper and Views of *The People* and compose them into an independent Nation.

The Colonies had grown up under Constitutions of Government so different, there was so great a variety of Religions, they were composed of so many different Nations, their Customs, Manners and Habits had so little resemblance, and their Intercourse had been so rare and their Knowledge of each other so imperfect, that to unite them in the Same Principles in Theory and the same System of Action was certainly a very difficult Enterprize. The compleat Accomplishment of it, in so short a time and by such simple means, was perhaps a singular Example in the History of Mankind. Thirteen Clocks were made to strike together, a perfection of Mechanism which no Artist had ever before effected.

In this Research, the Glorioroles [glorioles] of Individual Gentlemen and of separate States is of little Consequence. The MEANS AND THE MEASURES are the proper Objects of Investigation. These may be of Use to Posterity, not only in this Nation, but in South America, and all other Countries. They may teach Mankind that Revolutions are no Trifles; that they ought never to be undertaken rashly; nor without deliberate Consideration and sober Reflection; nor without a solid immutable, eternal foundation of Justice and Humanity; nor without a People posses[s]ed of Intelligenc[e], Fortitude and Integrity sufficient to carry them with Steadiness, Patience, and Perseverance, through all the Vicissitudes of fortune, the fiery Tryals and melancholly Disasters they may have to encounter.

The Town of Boston early instituted an annual Oration on the fourth of July, in commemoration of the Principles and Feelings which contributed to produce the Revolution. Many of those Orations I have heard, and all that I could obtain I have read. Much Ingenuity and Eloquence appears upon every Subject, except those Principles and Feelings. That of my honest and amiable Neighbour, Josiah Quincy, appeared to me, the most directly to the purpose of the Institution. Those Principles and Feelings ought to be traced back for Two hundred Years, and sought in the history of the Country from the first Plantations in America. Nor should the Principles and Feelings of the English and Scotch towards the Colonies, through that whole Period ever be forgotten. The perpetual discordance between British Principles and Feelings and those of America, the next Year after the Suppression of the French Power in America, came to a Crisis, and produced an Explosion.

It was not till after the Annihilation of the French Dominion in America, that any British Ministry had dared to gratify their own Wishes, and the desire of the Nation, by projecting a formal Plan for raising a national Revenue from America by Parliamentary Taxation. The first great manifestation of this design, was by the Order to carry into strict Executions those Acts of Parliament which were well known by the Appelation of the *Acts of Trade*, which had lain a dead Letter, unexecuted for half a Century, and some of them I believe for nearly a whole one.

This produced, in 1760 and 1761, AN AWAKENING and a REVIVAL of American Principles and Feelings, with an Enthusiasm which went on increasing till in 1775 it burst out in open Violence, Hostility and Fury.

2

Thomas Hutchinson
"They came, with intoxicated rage,
upon the house of the lieutenant-governor"

Thomas Hutchinson, the last royal governor of Massachusetts, wrote a three-volume history of Massachusetts, of which the third volume, not to be published until 1828 after the author's death, was concerned with the revolutionary period. In this work Hutchinson imputed ignoble motives to revolutionary leaders, emphasized the influence of radical propaganda on the people, and argued that fear of British intentions toward the colonies was an important cause of the Revolution. Although he had been intimately involved in the events leading to the outbreak of the war, Hutchinson's History *maintained a remarkably temperate tone. This is well shown by the following passage in which Hutchinson details the reaction of Boston to the Stamp Act, including the sacking by a mob of his own house, and the narrow escape of himself and family.*

There appeared to be a general determination, among the people, to prevent the execution of the stamp act, if possible; but there did not appear to be any plan concerted. Most people of judgment thought that it would force its way; but it did not.

The first act of any of the assemblies, against the authority of

SOURCE. Thomas Hutchinson, *The History of the Colony and Province of Massachusetts-Bay,* ed. by Lawrence Shaw Mayo. Cambridge, Mass.: Harvard University Press, 1936, **III,** 86–91. Copyright 1936, 1964, by the President and Fellows of Harvard College. Reprinted by permission of the publishers.

the act of parliament, was in Virginia. These resolves were expressed in such terms that many people, upon the first surprise, pronounced them treasonable. But the astonishment was of no long duration. The newspapers soon vindicated the resolves. From having been censured, the spirit discovered in them was applauded, as worthy of imitation; and the declaration in them, that all who maintained the right of parliament should be deemed enemies to the colony, had a tendency to bring on those acts of violence which soon after were committed in Boston.

The distributor of stamps for the colony of Connecticut arrived in Boston from London; and, having been agent for that colony, and in other respects of a very reputable character, received from many gentlemen of the town such civilities as were due to him. When he set out for Connecticut, Mr. Oliver, the distributor for Massachusetts Bay, accompanied him out of town. This occasioned murmuring among the people, and an inflammatory piece in the next Boston Gazette. A few days after, early in the morning, a stuffed image was hung upon a tree, called the great tree of the south part of Boston. Labels affixed denoted it to be designed for the distributor of stamps. People, who were passing by, stopped to view it, and the report caused others to gather from all quarters of the town, and many from the towns adjacent. The governor caused the council to be convened. Before they came to any determination, the sheriff, with his deputies, had been to the place, but, by advice of some of the graver persons present, forbore any attempt to remove the image. The majority of the council, but not the whole, advised not to meddle with it; and urged as a reason, that the people were orderly, and, if left alone, would take down the image, and bury it without any disturbance; but an attempt to remove it would bring on a riot, the mischief designed to be prevented.

The governor, however, thought fit to meet the council again in the afternoon. Before night, the image was taken down, and carried through the townhouse, in the chamber whereof the governor and council were sitting. Forty or fifty tradesmen, decently dressed, preceded; and some thousands of the mob followed down King street to Oliver's dock, near which Mr. Oliver had lately erected a building, which, it was conjectured, he designed for a stamp office. This was laid flat to the ground in a few minutes. From thence the mob proceeded for Fort Hill, but Mr. Oliver's house being in the way, they endeavoured to force themselves into it, and being opposed, broke the windows, beat down the doors, entered, and destroyed part of his furniture, and continued in riot until midnight, before they separated.

The next day, the governor, by advice of council, issued a proclamation, offering a reward for discovering offenders, &c. Many of the offenders were known, and the proclamation was considered as a mere matter of form. Some of the council advised to a military watch in the town the next night, but a majority were against it, and thought it enough to recommend to the select men and justices, to increase the number of the ordinary town watch; but even this was not done. Several of the council gave it as their opinion, Mr. Oliver being present, that the people, not only of the town of Boston, but of the country in general, would never submit to the execution of the stamp act, let the consequence of an opposition to it be what it would. It was also reported, that the people of Connecticut had threatened to hang their distributor on the first tree after he entered the colony; and that, to avoid it, he had turned aside to Rhode-Island.

Despairing of protection, and finding his family in terror and great distress, Mr. Oliver came to a sudden resolution to resign his office before another night, and immediately signified, by a writing under his hand, to one of his friends, that he would send letters, by a ship then ready to sail for London, which should contain such resignation; and he desired that the town might be made acquainted with it, and with the strong assurances he had given, that he would never act in that capacity.

This victory was matter of triumph. The mob assembled in the evening; not to insult the distributor, but to give him thanks, and to make a bonfire upon the hill near his house.

It was hoped that the people, having obtained all that they desired, would return to order, but, having repeatedly assembled with impunity, a very small pretence served to induce them to re-assemble.

The next evening, the mob surrounded the house of the lieutenant-governor and chief justice. He was at Mr. Oliver's house when it was assaulted, and had excited the sheriff, and the colonel of the regiment, to attempt to suppress the mob. A report was soon spread, that he was a favourer of the stamp act, and had encouraged it by letters to the ministry. Upon notice of the approach of the people, he caused the doors and windows to be barred; and remained in the house. After attempting to enter, they called upon him to come into the balcony, and to declare that he had not written in favour of the act, and they would retire quite satisfied. This was an indignity to which he would not submit; and, therefore, he made no answer. An ancient reputable tradesman obtained their attention, and endeavoured to persuade them, not only of the unwarrantableness of their proceedings, but of the groundlessness of their suspicions of the lieutenant-governor, who might well enough wish the act of parliament had not passed, though he disapproved of the violent opposition to its execution. Some were for withdrawing, and others for continuing; when one of the neighbours called to them from his window and affirmed, that he saw the lieutenant-governor in his carriage, just before night, and that he was gone to lodge at his house in the country. Upon this, they dispersed, with only breaking some of the glass.

These attacks upon two of the principal officers of the crown struck terror into people of inferior rank; and though they saw the danger from this assumed power in the populace, yet they would give no aid in discountenancing it, lest they should become obnoxious themselves; for there were whisperings of danger from further acts of violence. On Sunday the 25th of August, a sermon was preached, in what was called the West meeting-house, from these words, "I would they were even cut off which trouble you." The text alone, without a comment, delivered from the pulpit at that time, might be construed by some of the auditory into an approbation of the prevailing irregularities. One, who had a chief hand in the outrages which soon followed, declared, when he was in prison, that he was excited to them by this sermon, and that he thought he was doing God service.

Certain depositions had been taken, many months before these transactions, by order of the governor, concerning the illicit trade carrying on; and one of them, made by the judge of the admiralty, at the special desire of the governor, had been sworn to before the lieutenant-governor, as chief justice. They had been shewn, at one of the offices in England, to a person who arrived in Boston just at this time, and he had acquainted several merchants, whose names were in some of the depositions as smugglers, with the contents. This brought, though without reason, the resentment of the merchants against the persons who, by their office, were obliged to administer the oaths, as well as against the officers of the customs and admiralty, who had made the depositions; and the leaders of the mob contrived a riot, which, after some small efforts against such officers, was to spend its principal force upon the lieutenant-governor. And, in the evening of the 26th of August, such a mob was collected in King street, drawn there by a bonfire, and well supplied with strong drink. After some annoyance to the house of the registrar of the admiralty, and somewhat greater to that of the comptroller of the customs, whose cellars they plundered of the wine and spirits in them, they came, with intoxicated rage, upon the house of the lieutenant-governor. The doors were immediately split to pieces with broad axes, and a way made there, and at the windows, for the entry of the mob; which poured in, and filled, in an instant, every room in the house.

The lieutenant-governor had very short notice of the approach of the mob. He directed his children, and the rest of his family, to leave the house immediately, determining to keep possession himself. His eldest daughter, after going a little way from the house, returned, and refused to quit it, unless her father would do the like.

This caused him to depart from his resolution, a few minutes before the mob entered. They continued their possession until daylight; destroyed, carried away, or cast into the street, every thing that was in the house; demolished every part of it, except the walls, as far as lay in their power; and had begun to break away the brick-work.

The damage was estimated at about twenty-five hundred pounds sterling, without any regard to a great collection of publick as well as private papers, in the possession and custody of the lieutenant-governor.

The town was, the whole night, under the awe of this mob; many of the magistrates, with the field officers of the militia, standing by as spectators; and no body daring to oppose, or contradict.

The governor was at the castle, and knew nothing of what had happened until the next morning. He then went to town, and caused a council to be summoned. Before they could meet, the inhabitants of Boston assembled in Faneuil Hall; and, in as full a meeting as had been known, by an unanimous vote, declared an utter detestation of the extraordinary and violent proceedings of a number of persons unknown, against some of the inhabitants of the town, the preceding night; and desired the select men, and magistrates of the town, to use their utmost endeavours to suppress the like disorders for the future; the freeholders, and other inhabitants, being ready to do every thing in their power to assist them. It could not be doubted, that many of those who were immediate actors in, as well as of those who had been abettors of, those violent proceedings, were present at this unanimous vote.

The council advised a proclamation, with promise of 300*l.* reward for discovering the leader or leaders, and 100*l*, for every other person. Information had been before given to the justices of peace in the town, and warrants had been issued and delivered to the sheriff for apprehending several persons. One of them, a tradesman of the town, whose name was Mackintosh, was soon taken in King street; but the sheriff was immediately surrounded by a number of merchants, and other persons of property and character, who assured him, that, if he apprehended Mackintosh, not a man would appear in arms, as had been proposed, for the security of the town the next night. The sheriff released him, and made return of his doings to the governor, then in council. Some of the council gave their opinion, that the sheriff was inexcusable; but it passed over without any act of council to shew a disapprobation. To this feeble state were the powers of government reduced.

Six or eight other persons were apprehended, and, upon examination, committed to prison in order to trial, and were generally considered as capital offenders. Before the time of trial, a considerable number of people entered the house of the prison-keeper late in the evening, compelled him, by threats, to deliver to them the keys of the prison, which they opened, and then set the prisoners at liberty; and all this without any tumult. The prisoners thought fit to disappear for some months; but there was no authority, which considered it advisable to make any inquiry after them.

3

David Ramsay
"It seemed as if the war not only required, but created talents"

David Ramsay, born in Pennsylvania and educated at the College of New Jersey (now Princeton University), became a doctor in Charleston, South Carolina. He also turned to politics, served first in the state legislature, and later in the Continental Congresses of 1782–1783 and 1785–1786.

Although Ramsay's History of the American Revolution *was basically political and constitutional, it showed for his time a striking awareness of economic and social factors, including such influences in history as religious traditions, national origins, age, education, the impetus political activity gave to creative work, and the psychological effects of fear and hope. In the following extract, concerned with the consequences of the Revolution, one is sometimes reminded of J. Franklin Jameson's* The American Revolution Considered as a Social Movement *(1926).*

Previous to the American revolution, the inhabitants of the British colonies were universally loyal. That three millions of such subjects should break through all former attachments, and unanimously adopt new ones, could not reasonably be expected. The revolution had its enemies, as well as its friends, in every

SOURCE. David Ramsay, *The History of the American Revolution.* Philadelphia: R. Aitken & Son, 1789, II, 310–325.

period of the war. Country religion, local policy, as well as private views, operated in disposing the inhabitants to take different sides. The New-England provinces being mostly settled by one sort of people, were nearly of one sentiment. The influence of placemen in Boston, together with the connexions which they had formed by marriages, had attached sundry influential characters in that capital to the British interest, but these were but as the dust in the balance, when compared with the numerous independent whig yeomanry of the country. The same and other causes produced a large number in New-York, who were attached to royal government. That city had long been head quarters of the British army in America, and many intermarriages, and other connexions, had been made between British officers, and some of their first families. The practice of entailing estates had prevailed in New-York to a much greater extent, than in any of the other provinces. The governors thereof had long been in the habit of indulging their favorites with extravagant grants of land. This had introduced the distinction of landlord and tenant. There was therefore in New-York an aristocratic party, respectable for numbers, wealth and influence, which had much to fear from independence. The city was also divided into parties by the influence of two ancient and numerous families, the Livingstones and Delanceys. These having been long accustomed to oppose each other at elections, could rarely be brought to unite, in any political measures. In this controversy, one almost universally took part with America, the other with Great Britain.

The Irish in America, with a few exceptions were attached to independence. They had fled from oppression in their native country, and could not brook the idea that it should follow them. Their national prepossessions in favour of liberty, were strengthened by their religious opinions. They were Presbyterians, and people of that denomination, for reasons hereafter to be explained, were mostly whigs. The Scotch on the other hand, though they had formerly sacrificed much to liberty in their own country, were generally disposed to support the claims of Great-Britain. Their nation for some years past had experienced a large proportion of royal favour. A very absurd association was made by many, between the cause of John Wilkes and the cause of America. The former had rendered himself so universally odious to the Scotch, that many of them were prejudiced against a cause, which was so ridiculously, but generally associated, with that of a man who had grossly insulted their whole nation. The illiberal reflections cast by some Americans on the whole body of the Scotch, as favourers of arbitrary power, restrained high spirited individuals of that nation, from joining a people who suspected their love of liberty. Such of them as adhered to the cause of independence, were steady in their attachment. The army and the Congress ranked among their best officers, and most valuable members, some individuals of that nation.

Such of the Germans, in America, as possessed the means of information, were generally determined whigs, but many of them were too little informed, to be able to chuse their side on proper ground. They, especially such of them as resided in the interior country, were from their not understanding the English language, far behind most of the other inhabitants, in a knowledge of the merits of the dispute. Their disaffection was rather passive than active: A considerable part of it arose from principles of religion, for some of their sects deny the lawfulness of war. No people have prospered more in America than the Germans. None have surpassed, and but few have equalled them, in industry and other republican virtues.

The great body of tories in the southern states, was among the settlers on their western frontier. Many of these were disorderly persons, who had fled from the old settlements, to avoid the restraints of civil government. Their numbers were increased by a set of men called regulators. The expence and difficulty of obtaining the decision of courts, against horse-thieves and other criminals, had induced sundry persons, about the year 1770, to take the execution of the laws into their own hands, in some of the remote settlements, both of North and South-Carolina. In punishing crimes, forms as well as substance, must be regarded. From not attending to the former, some of these regulators, though perhaps aiming at nothing but what they thought right, committed many offences both against law and justice. By their violent proceedings regular government was prostrated. This drew on them the vengeance of royal governors. The regulators having suffered from their hands, were slow to oppose an established government, whose power to punish they had recently experienced. Apprehending that the measures of Congress were like their own regulating schemes, and fearing that they would terminate in the same disagreeable consequences, they and their adherents were generally opposed to the revolution.

Religion also divided the inhabitants of America. The presbyterians and independents, were almost universally attached to the measures of Congress. Their religious societies are governed on the republican plan.

From independence they had much to hope, but from Great Britain if finally successful, they had reason to fear the establishment of a church hierarchy. Most of the episcopal ministers of the northern provinces, were pensioners on the bounty of the British government. The greatest part of their clergy, and many of their laity in these provinces, were therefore disposed to support a connexion with Great Britain. The episcopal clergy in these southern provinces being under no such bias, were often among the warmest whigs. Some of them foreseeing the downfall of religious establishments from the success of the Americans, were less active, but in general where their church was able to support itself, their clergy and laity, zealously espoused the cause of independence. Great pains were taken to persuade them, that those who had been called dissenters, were aiming to abolish the espiscopal establishment, to make way for their own exaltation, but the good sense of the people, restrained them from giving any credit to the unfounded suggestion. Religious controversy was happily kept out of view: The well informed of all denominations were convinced, that the contest was for their civil rights, and therefore did not suffer any other considerations to interfere, or disturb their union.

The quakers with a few exceptions were averse to independence. In Pennsylvania they were numerous, and had power in their hands. Revolutions in government are rarely patronised by any body of men, who foresee that a diminution of their own importance, is likely to result from the change. Quakers from religious principles were averse to war, and therefore could not be friendly to a revolution, which could only be effected by the sword. Several individuals separated from them on account of their principles, and following the impulse of their inclinations, joined their countrymen in arms. The services America received from two of their society, Generals Greene and Mifflin, made some amends for the embarrassment, which the disaffection of the great body of their people occasioned to the exertions of the active friends of independence.

The age and temperament of individuals had often an influence in fixing their political character. Old man were seldom warm whigs. They could not relish the great changes which were daily taking place. Attached to ancient forms and habits, they could not readily accommodate themselves to new systems. Few of the very rich were active in forwarding the revolution. This was remarkably the case in the eastern and middle States; but the reverse took place in the southern extreme of the confederacy. There were in no part of America, more determined whigs than the opulent slaveholders in Virginia, the Carolinas and Georgia. The active and spirited part of the community, who felt themselves possessed of talents, that would raise them to eminence in a free government, longed for the establishment of independent constitutions: But those who were in possession or expectation of royal favour, or of promotion from Great Britain, wished that the connexion between the Parent State and the colonies, might be preserved. The young, the ardent, the ambitious and the enterprising were mostly whigs, but the phlegmatic, the timid, the interested and those who wanted decision were, in general, favourers of Great Britain, or at least only the lukewarm inactive friends of independence. The whigs received a great reinforcement from the operation of continental money. In the year 1775, 1776, and in the first months of 1777, while the bills of Congress were in good credit, the effects of them were the same, as it a foreign power had made the United States a present of twenty million of silver dollars. The circulation of so large a sum of money, and the employment given to great numbers in providing for the American army, increased the numbers and invigorated the zeal of the friends to the revolution: on the same principles, the American war was patronised in England, by the many contractors and agents for transporting and supplying the British army. In both cases the inconveniences of interrupted commerce were lessened by the employment which war and a domestic circulation of money substituted in its room. The convulsions of war afforded excellent shelter for desperate debtors. The spirit of the times revolted against dragging to jails for debt, men who were active and zealous in defending their country, and on the other hand, those who owed more than they were worth, by going within the British lines, and giving themselves the merit of suffering on the score of loyalty, not only put their creditors to defiance, but sometimes obtained promotion or other special marks of royal favour.

The American revolution, on the one hand, brought forth great vices; but on the other hand, it called forth many virtues, and gave occasion for the display of abilities which, but for that event, would have been lost to the world. When the war began, the Americans were a mass of husbandmen, merchants, mechanics and fishermen; but the necessities of the country gave a spring to the active powers of the inhabitants, and set them on thinking, speaking and acting, in a line far beyond that to which they had been accustomed. The difference between nations is not so much owing to nature, as to education and circumstances. While the Americans were guided by the leading strings of the mother country, they had no scope nor encouragement for exertion. All the departments of government were established and executed for them, but not by them. In the years 1775 and 1776 the country, being suddenly thrown into a situation that needed the abilities of all its sons, these generally took their places, each according to the bent of his inclination. As they severally pursued their objects with ardor, a vast expansion of the human mind speedily followed. This displayed itself in a variety of ways. It was found that the talents for great stations did not differ in kind, but only in degree, from those which were necessary for the proper discharge of the ordinary business of civil society. In the bustle that was occasioned by the war, few instances could be produced of any persons who made a figure, or who rendered essential services, but from among those who had given specimens of similar talents in their respective professions. Those who from indolence or dissipation, had been of little service to the community in time of peace, were found equally unserviceable in war. A few young men were exceptions to this general rule. Some of these, who had indulged in youthful follies, broke off from their vicious courses, and on the pressing call of their country became useful servants of the public: but the great bulk of those, who were the active instruments of carrying on the revolution, were self-made, industrious men. Those who by their own exertions, had established or laid a foundation for establishing personal independence, were most generally trusted, and most successfully employed in establishing that of their country. In these times of action, classical education was found of less service than good natural parts, guided by common sense and sound judgement.

Several names could be mentioned of individuals who, without the knowledge of any other language than their mother tongue, wrote not only accurately, but elegantly, on public business. It seemed as if the war not only required, but created talents. Men whose minds were warmed with the love of liberty, and whose abilities were improved by daily exercise, and sharpened with a laudable ambition to serve their distressed country, spoke, wrote, and acted, with an energy far surpassing all expectations which could be reasonably founded on their previous acquirements.

The Americans knew but little of one another, previous to the revolution. Trade and business had brought the inhabitants of their seaports acquainted with each other, but the bulk of the people in the interior country were unacquainted with their fellow citizens. A continental army, and Congress composed of men from all the States, by freely mixing together, were assimilated into one mass. Individuals of both, mingling with the citizens, disseminated principles of union among them. Local prejudices abated. By frequent collision asperities were worn off, and a foundation was laid for the establishment of a nation, out of discordant materials. Intermarriages between men and women of different States were much more common than before the war, and became an additional cement to the union. Unreasonable jealous[i]es had existed between the inhabitants of the eastern and of the southern States; but on becoming better acquainted with each other, these in a great measure subsided. A wiser policy prevailed. Men of liberal minds led the way in discouraging local distinctions, and the great body of the people, as soon as reason got the better of prejudice, found that their best interests would be most effectually promoted by such practices and sentiments as were favourable to union. Religious bigotry had broken in upon the peace of various sects, before the American war. This was kept up by partial establishments, and by a dread that the church of England through the power of the mother country, would be made to triumph over all other denominations. These apprehensions were done away by the revolution. The different sects, having nothing to fear from each other, dismissed all religious controversy. A proposal for introducing bishops into America before the war, had kindled a flame among the dissenters; but the revolution was no sooner accomplished, than a scheme for that purpose was perfected, with the consent and approbation of all those sects who had previously opposed it. Pulpits which had formerly been shut to worthy men, because their heads had not been consecrated by the imposition of the hands of a bishop or of a Presbytery, have since the establishment of independence, been reciprocally opened to each other, whensoever the public convenience required it. The world will soon see the result of an experiment in politics, and be able to determine whether the happiness of society is increased by religious establishments, or diminished by the want of them.

Though schools and colleges were generally shut up during the war, yet many of the arts and sciences were promoted by it. The Geography of the United States before the revolution was but little known; but the marches of armies, and the operations of war, gave birth to many geographical enquiries and discoveries, which otherwise would not have been made. A passionate fondness for studies of this kind, and the growing importance of the country, excited one of its sons, the Rev. Mr. Morse, to travel through every State of the Union, and amass a fund of topographical knowledge far exceeding any thing heretofore communicated to the public. The necessities of the States led to the study of Tactics, Fortification, Gunnery, and a variety of other arts connected with war, and diffused a knowledge of them among a peaceable people, who would otherwise have had no inducement to study them.

The abilities of ingenious men were directed to make farther improvements in the art of destroying an enemy. Among these, David Bushnell of Connecticut invented a machine for submarine navigation, which was found to answer the purpose of rowing horizontally, at any given depth under water, and of rising or sinking at pleasure. To this was attached a magazine of powder, and the whole was contrived in such a manner, as to make it practicable to blow up vessels by machinery under them. Mr. Bushnell also contrived sundry other curious machines for the annoyance of British shipping; but from accident they only succeeded in part. He destroyed one vessel in charge of Commodore Symonds, and a second one near the shore of Long-Island.

Surgery was one of the arts which was promoted by the war. From the want of hospitals and other aids, the medical men of America, had few opportunities of perfecting themselves in this art, the thorough knowledge of which can only be acquired by practice and observation. The melancholy events of battles, gave the American students an opportunity of seeing, and learning more in one day, than they could have acquired in years of peace. It was in the hospitals of the United States, that Dr. Rush first discovered the method of curing the lock jaw by bark and wine, added to other invigorating remedies, which has since been adopted with success in Europe, as well as in the United States.

The science of government, has been more generally diffused among the Americans by means of the revolution. The policy of Great Britain, in throwing them out of her protection, induced a necessity of establishing independent constitutions. This led to reading and reasoning on the subject. The many errors that were at first committed by unexperienced statesmen, have been a practical comment on the folly of unbalanced constitutions, and injudicious laws. The discussions concerning the new constitution, gave birth to much reasoning on the subject of government, and particularly to a series of letters signed Publius, but really the work of Alexander Hamilton, in which such political knowledge and wisdom were displayed, and which will long remain a monument of the strength and acuteness of the human understanding in investigating truth.

4   *George Bancroft*
"With one heart, the continent cried: 'Liberty or Death' "

George Bancroft's career and writings span most of the nineteenth century. Born in Massachusetts in 1800, he was graduated from Harvard College in 1817 and then studied at the University of Gottingen. Back in the United States, he became a powerful figure in the Democratic Party and was in time appointed Secretary of Navy as a reward for having helped Polk to win the nomination for president.

Bancroft's History of the United States *was the product of immense research—an effort that was eased by the author's wealth and political and diplomatic connections. The following passage is from "The Author's Last Revision" (1883–1885) in which the style is somewhat less florid than in earlier editions. It nevertheless reveals Bancroft's ardent nationalism and the detailed but dramatic presentation that made his great history the object of American pride for half a century.*

Darkness closed upon the country and upon the town, but it was no night for sleep. Heralds by swift relays transmitted the war message from hand to hand, till village repeated it to village; the sea to the backwoods; the plains to the highlands; and it was never suffered to droop till it had been borne north and south, and east and west, throughout the land. It spread over the bays

SOURCE. George Bancroft, *History of the United States of America, from the Discovery of the Continent.* New York: D. Appleton and Co., 1884, IV, 167–174, 175–176.

that received the Saco and the Penobscot and the St. John's. Its loud reveille broke the rest of the trappers of New Hampshire, and, ringing like bugle-notes from peak to peak, overleapt the Green Mountains, swept onward to Montreal, and descended the ocean river, till the responses were echoed from the cliffs of Quebec. The hills along the Hudson told one to another the tale. As the summons hurried to the south, it was one day at New York; in one more at Philadelphia; the next it lighted a watchfire at Baltimore; thence it waked an answer at Annapolis. Crossing the Potomac near Mount Vernon, it was sent forward without a halt to Williamsburg. It traversed the Dismal Swamp to Nansemond along the route of the first emigrants to North Carolina. It moved onward and still onward through boundless forests of pines to Newbern and to Wilmington. "For God's sake, forward it by night and by day," wrote Cornelius Harnett by the express which sped for Brunswick. Patriots of South Carolina caught up its tones at the border, and despatched it to Charleston, and through moss-clad live oaks and palmettoes still farther to the south, till it resounded among the New England settlements beyond the Savannah. Hillsborough and the Mecklenburg district of North Carolina rose in triumph, now that their wearisome uncertainty had its end. The Blue Ridge took up the voice, and made it heard from one end to the other of the valley of Virginia. The Alleghanies opened their barriers, that the "loud call" might pass through to the hardy riflemen on the Holston, the Watauga, and the French Broad. Ever renewing its strength, powerful enough even to create a commonwealth, it breathed its inspiring word to the first settlers of Kentucky; so that hunters, who made their halt in the matchless valley of the Elkhorn, commemorated the nineteenth day of April by naming their encampment LEXINGTON.

With one impulse, the colonies sprung to arms; with one spirit, they pledged themselves to each other "to be ready for the extreme event." With one heart, the continent cried: "Liberty or Death."

The first measure of the Massachusetts committee of safety, after the dawn of the twentieth of April, was a circular to the several towns in Massachusetts. "We conjure you," they wrote, "by all that is dear, by all that is sacred; we beg and entreat, as you will answer it to your country, to your consciences, and, above all, to God himself, that you will hasten and encourage by all possible means the enlistment of men to form the army, and send them forward to head-quarters at Cambridge with that expedition which the vast importance and instant urgency of the affair demands."

The country people of Massachusetts had not waited for the call. As soon as they heard the cry of blood they snatched their firelocks from the walls, and wives and mothers and sisters took part in preparing the men of their households to go forth to the war. The farmers rushed to "the camp of liberty," often with nothing but the clothes on their backs, without a day's provisions, and many without a farthing in their pockets. Their country was in danger; their brethren were slaughtered; their arms alone employed their attention. On their way, the inhabitants opened their hospitable doors, and all things were in common. For the first night of the siege, Prescott of Pepperell, with his Middlesex minute-men, kept the watch over the entrance to Boston; and, while Gage was driven for safety to fortify the town at all points, the Americans talked of driving him and his regiments into the sea.

At the same time, the committee by letter gave the story of the preceding day to New Hampshire and Connecticut, whose assistance they entreated. "We shall be glad," they wrote, "that our brethren who come to our aid may be supplied with military stores and provisions, as we have none of either more than is absolutely necessary for ourselves." And without stores or cannon, or supplies even of powder, or of money, Massachusetts, by its congress, on the twenty-second of April, resolved unanimously that a New England army of thirty thousand men should be raised, and established its own proportion at thirteen thousand six hundred. The term of enlistment was fixed for the last day of December.

Long before this summons, the ferries over the Merrimack were crowded by men from New Hampshire. "We go," said they, "to the assistance of our brethren." By one o'clock of the twentieth, upward of sixty men of Nottingham assembled at the meeting-house with arms and equipments, under Cilley and Dearborn; before two, they were joined by bands from Deerfield and Epsom; and they set out together for Cambridge. At dusk they reached Haverhill ferry, a distance of twenty-seven miles, having run rather than marched; they halted in Andover only for refreshments, and, traversing fifty-five miles in less than twenty hours, by sunrise of the twenty-first paraded on Cambridge common.

The veteran John Stark, skilled in the ways of the Indian, the English, and his countrymen, able to take his rest on a bear-skin with a bank of snow for a pillow, frank and humane, eccentric but true, famed for coolness and courage and integrity, had no rival in the confidence of his neighbors, and was chosen colonel of their regiment by their unanimous vote. He rode in haste to the scene of action, on the way encouraging the volunteers to rendezvous at Medford. So many followed that, on the morning of the twenty-second, he was detached with three hundred to take post at Chelsea, where his battalion, which was one of the fullest in the besieging army, became a model for its discipline.

By the twenty-third there were already about two thousand men from the interior parts of New Hampshire, desirous "not to return before the work was done." Many who remained near the upper Connecticut threw up the civil and military commissions held from the king; for, said they, "the king has forfeited his crown, and all commissions from him are therefore vacated."

In Connecticut, Trumbull, the governor, sent out writs to convene the legislature of the colony at Hartford on the Wednesday following the battle. On the morning of the twentieth, Israel Putnam of Pomfret, in leather frock and apron, was assisting hired men to build a stone wall on his farm, when he heard the cry from Lexington. He set off instantly to rouse the militia officers of the nearest towns. On his return, he found hundreds who had mustered and chosen him their leader. Issuing orders for them to follow, he pushed forward without changing the check shirt he had worn in the field, and reached Cambridge at sunrise the next morning, having ridden the same horse a hundred miles within eighteen hours. He brought to the service of his country courage, and a heart than which none throbbed more honestly or warmly for American freedom.

From Wethersfield a hundred young volunteers marched for

Boston on the twenty-second, well armed and in high spirits. From the neighboring towns men of the largest estates, and the most esteemed for character, seized their firelocks and followed. By the second night, several thousands from the colony were on their way. Some had fixed on their standards and drums the colony arms, and round it, in letters of gold, the motto, that God who brought over their fathers would sustain the sons.

In New Haven, Benedict Arnold, captain of a volunteer company, agreed with his men to march the next morning for Boston. "Wait for proper orders," was the advice of Wooster; but their self-willed commander, brooking no delay, extorted supplies from the committee of the town, and on the twenty-ninth reached the American head-quarters with his company. There was scarcely a town in Connecticut that was not represented among the besiegers.

The nearest towns of Rhode Island were in motion before the British had finished their retreat. At the instance of Hopkins and others, Wanton, the governor, though himself inclined to the royal side, called an assembly. Its members were all of one mind; and when Wanton, with several of the council, showed hesitation, they resolved, if necessary, to proceed alone. The council yielded, and confirmed the unanimous vote of the assembly for raising an army of fifteen hundred men. "The colony of Rhode Island," wrote Bowler, the speaker, to the Massachusetts congress, "is firm and determined; and a greater unanimity in the lower house scarce ever prevailed." Companies of the men of Rhode Island preceded this early message.

Massachusetts gained confidence now that New Hampshire and Connecticut and Rhode Island had come to its support. The New England volunteers were men of substantial worth, of whom almost every one represented a household. The members of the several companies were well known to each other, as to brothers, kindred, and townsmen; known to the old men who remained at home, and to all the matrons and maidens. They were sure to be remembered weekly in the exercises of the congregations; and morning and evening, in the usual family devotions, they were commended with fervent piety to the protection of heaven. Every young soldier lived and acted, as it were, under the keen observation of all those among whom he had grown up, and was sure that his conduct would occupy the tongues of his village companions while he was in the field, and be remembered his life long. The camp of liberty was a gathering in arms of schoolmates, neighbors, and friends; and Boston was beleaguered round from Roxbury to Chelsea by an unorganized, fluctuating mass of men, each with his own musket and his little store of cartridges, and such provisions as he brought with him, or as were sent after him, or could be contributed by the people round about.

The British officers, from their own weakness and from fear of the American marksmen, dared not order a sally. Their confinement was the more irksome, for it came of a sudden before their magazines had been filled, and was followed by "an immediate stop to supplies of every kind." They had scoffed at the Americans as cowards who would run at their sight; and they had saved themselves only by the rapidity of their retreat. Re-enforcements and three new general officers were already on the Atlantic, and these would have to be received into straitened quarters by a defeated army. England, and even the ministers, would condemn the inglorious expedition which had brought about so sudden and so fatal a change. The officers shrunk from avowing their own acts; and, though no one would say that he had seen the Americans fire first, they tried to make it pass current that a handful of countrymen at Lexington had begun a fight with a detachment that outnumbered them as twelve to one.

The Americans, slowly provoked and long-suffering, treated the prisoners with tenderness, nursed the wounded as though they had been kinsmen, and invited Gage to send out British surgeons for their relief. Yet Percy could degrade himself so far as to calumniate the country people who gave him chase, and officially lend himself to the falsehood that "the rebels scalped and cut off the ears of some of the wounded who fell into their hands." He should have respected the name which he bore; and he should have respected the men before whom he fled.

To the inhabitants of Boston, Gage made the offer that, if they would promise not to join in an attack on his troops, and would lodge their arms with the selectmen at Faneuil Hall, the men, women, and children, with all their effects, should have safe conduct out of the town. The proposal was accepted. For several days the road to Roxbury was thronged with wagons and trains of exiles; but they were not allowed to take with them any food. The provincial congress devised measures for distributing five thousand of the poor among the villages of the interior. But the loyalists of Boston, of whom two hundred entered the king's service, soon prevailed with Gage to violate his word.

On the twenty-seventh of April the assembly of Connecticut read the vote of Massachusetts, that New England should bring into the field thirty thousand men. On the next day they despatched two envoys to Gage to plead for peace, yet to assure him of their most firm resolution to defend their rights to the last extremity and to aid their brethren. The mission was fruitless; but in the mean time the populous colony made ready to treat with sword in hand.

In the American camp there was no unity. At Roxbury, John Thomas had commanded, and received encomiums for the good order which prevailed in his division; but Ward, the general who was at Cambridge, had the virtues of a magistrate rather than of a soldier. He was old, unused to a separate military command, too infirm to appear on horseback, and wanting in "quick decision and activity." The troops from other colonies, under leaders of their own, did not as yet form an integral part of one "grand American" army.

Of the Massachusetts volunteers, the number varied from day to day. Many of them returned home almost as soon as they came, for want of provisions or clothes, or from the pressure of affairs which they had left so suddenly. Of those who enlisted in the Massachusetts army, a very large number absented themselves on furlough. Ward feared that he should be left alone. Of artillery, there were no more than six three-pounders and one six-pounder in Cambridge, besides sixteen pieces in Watertown, of different sizes, some of them good for nothing. There was no ammunition but for the six three-pounders, and very little even for them. After scouring five principal counties, the whole amount of powder that could be found was less than sixty-eight barrels. The other colonies were equally unprovided. In the colony of New York there were not more than one hundred pounds of powder for sale.

Notwithstanding these obstacles, the scheming genius of New England was in the highest activity. While the expedition against Ticonderoga was sanctioned by a commission granted to Benedict Arnold, the Massachusetts congress, which was then sitting in Watertown, received from Jonathan Brewer, of Waltham, a proposition to march with a body of five hundred volunteers to Quebec, by way of the rivers Kennebec and Chandière, in order to draw the governor of Canada, with his troops, into that quarter, and thus secure the northern and western frontiers from inroads. He was sure it "could be executed with all the facility imaginable." The design did not pass out of mind. . . .

On the fifth of May the provincial congress resolved "that General Gage had disqualified himself for serving the colony in any capacity; that no obedience was in future due to him; that he ought to be guarded against as an unnatural and in-veterate enemy." To take up the powers of civil government was an instant necessity; but the patriots of the colony checked their eagerness to return to their ancient custom of annually electing their chief magistrate, and resolved to await "explicit advice" from the continental congress.

New Hampshire agreed to raise two thousand men, of whom perhaps twelve hundred reached the camp. Folsom was their brigadier, but John Stark was the most trusty officer. Con-necticut offered six thousand men; and about twenty-three hun-dred remained at Cambridge, with Spenser as their chief, and Putnam as second brigadier.

Rhode Island voted fifteen hundred men; and probably about a thousand of them appeared round Boston, under Nathaniel Greene.

5   *Charles M. Andrews*

Revolutions "are the detonations of explosive materials, long accumulating and often long dormant"

Charles M. Andrews, the greatest figure among the imperalist historians, taught at Yale University from 1910 until 1931, after which he published his major work, The Colonial Period of American History *(4 vols., 1934-1938), a study that was only indirectly related to the American Revolution. Earlier, while still at Yale, he had written* The Colonial Background of the American Revolution *(1924), and in 1925 he delivered the presidential address to the American Historical Association on the American Revolution, reprinted here.*

The pro-British bias and the admiration for eighteenth-century imperial administration shown by some of the imperialist historians find no support in this article by Andrews. Between England's "immutable, stereotyped system" and that of America, "a vital, dynamic organism, containing the seed of a great nation, its forces untried, still to be proved," conflict seemed inevitable.

You will not, I trust, take it amiss if, on this the occasion of our annual meeting, I select as my topic the familiar subject of the American Revolution. Quite apart from the pleasure

SOURCE. Charles M. Andrews, "The American Revolution: An Interpretation," *American Historical Review,* 31 (January 1926), 219–232. Reprinted by permission of the American Historical Association.

that comes from harping on an old string, there is the conviction, which I hold very strongly, that no matter how familiar a subject may be, it can always be re-examined with profit and viewed not infrequently from such points of vantage as to set the scene in quite a new light. The writing of history is always a progressive process, not merely or mainly because each age must write its own history from its own point of view, but rather because each generation of scholars is certain to contribute to historical knowledge and so to approach nearer than its predecessor to an understanding of the past. No one can accept as complete or final any rendering of history, no matter how plausible it may be, nor consider any period or phase of the past as closed against further investigation. Our knowledge of history is and always will be in the making, and it has been well said that orthodox history and an orthodox historian involve a contradiction in terms.

The explanations of history have been characterized as a rule by overmuch simplicity. So wrote Maitland of the history of England and so with equal justice might he have written of the history of America. As with natural phenomena in the pre-Copernican days of celestial mechanics, when the world believed that the sun moved and the earth was flat, so it has been at all times with historical phenomena, that what to the superficial observer has appeared to be true has been accepted far too often as containing the whole truth. Among these pre-Copernican convictions, for example, widely held in America to-day, is the belief that the American Revolution was brought about by British tyranny. Whatever explanation of that great event comes to be accepted by competent historians and their intelligent readers as a near approach to the truth, it is quite certain that it will not be anything as easy and simple as all that. There was nothing simple about the Balance of Power or the Balance of Trade, even when construed in terms of such vulgar commodities as fish, furs, and molasses, and particularly when one must give due consideration to the doctrine, as seriously held in some quarters today as it was in the eighteenth century, that colonial possessions are the natural sources for home industries. Our history before 1783 was a much more complex and cosmopolitan affair than older writers would have us believe, for they have failed to account for many deep-lying and almost invisible factors and forces which influence and often determine human action and are always elusive and difficult to comprehend.

Recent writers have approached the subject with a full recognition of the complexity of the problems involved. They have found many and varied conflicting activities making for disagreement and misunderstanding between the mother country and her offspring, giving rise to impulses and convictions, ideas and practices, that were difficult, if not impossible, of reconciliation. Such scholars have expressed their conclusions in many different forms. Some have seen a struggle between two opposing historical tendencies—one imperialistic and expansive, the other domestic and intensive; others, a clash of ideas regarding the constitution of the British empire and the place that a colony should occupy in its relations with the mother country. Some have stressed the differences that were bound to arise between an old and settled country and one that was not only dominated by the ideas and habits of the frontier, but was opposed also to the continued supremacy of a governing authority three thousand miles away. Others have explained the situation in terms of an antagonism between the law and institutions of England and those, growing constantly more divergent, of the Puritan and non-Puritan colonies in America. All of these explanations are sound, because they are based on an understanding of the deeper issues involved; and taken together, they are illuminating in that they enable the reader to broaden his point of view, and to break away from the endless controversies over immediate causes and war guilt that have hitherto tended to dominate the American mind.

But elucidating as these explanations are, no one of them seems quite sufficient to resolve so complex a subject as the causes of the American Revolution. To-day we conjure with such words as evolution and psychology, and look for explanations of acts on the part of both individuals and groups in states of mind produced by inheritance and environment. Fielding, acknowledged expert in the study of human experience, can say that for a man "to act in direct contradiction to the dictates of his nature is, if not impossible, as improbable as anything which can well be conceived". The philosophers tell us that mind can be more resistant even than matter, and that it is easier to remove mountains than it is to change the ideas of a people. That the impact of convictions is one of the most frequent causes of revolution we must acknowledge; and I believe that we have not considered sufficiently the importance of this fact in determining the relations of England with colonial America. If I may, by way of illustrating my point, I should like to show that certain differences existing between England and her colonies in mental attitudes and convictions proved in the end more difficult to overcome than the diverging historical tendencies or the bridging the three thousand miles of the Atlantic itself.

The American Revolution marks the close of one great period of our history and the beginning of another of even greater significance. It is the red line across our years, because by it was brought about a fundamental change in the status of the communities on the American seaboard—a change from dependence to independence. We sometimes hear that revolutions are not made but happen. In their immediate causes this is not true—for revolutions do not happen, they are made, in that they are the creatures of propaganda and manipulation. But, in reality, revolutions are not made. They are the detonations of explosive materials, long accumulating and often long dormant. They are the resultants of a vast complex of economic, political, social, and legal forces, which taken collectively are the masters, not the servants, of statesmen and political agitators. They are never sudden in their origin, but look back to influences long in the making; and it is the business of the modern student of the subject to discover those remoter causes and to examine thoroughly and with an open mind the history, institutions, and mental past of the parties to the conflict. In pursuit of my purpose let me call to your attention certain aspects of that most important of all periods of our early history, the years from 1713 to 1775 .

The middle period of the eighteenth century in England,

resembling in some respects the mid-Victorian era of the next century, was intellectually, socially, and institutionally in a state of stable equilibrium. The impulses of the Revolution of 1689 had spent their force. English thought and life was tending to become formal, conventional, and artificial, and the English mind was acquiring the fatal habit of closing against novelty and change. The most enlightened men of the day regarded the existing order as the best that could be conceived, and in the main were content to let well enough alone. Those who held the reins of power were comfortable and irresponsible, steeped in their "old vulgar prejudices", and addicted to habits and modes of living that were approved by age and precedent. The miseries of the poor were accepted as due to inherent viciousness; class distinctions were sharply marked, and social relations were cast in a rigid mould; while, as far as the mass of the poor was concerned, the vagrancy laws and the narrow policy of the corporate towns made free movement in any direction practically impossible. Life at large was characterized by brutality and a widespread sense of insecurity. Little thought was given to the education of the poor, the diseases of poverty and dirt, the baneful effects of overcrowding in the towns, or the corrupting influence of life in tenements and cellars. Excessive drinking and habitual resort to violence in human relations prevailed in urban sections; and while it is probably true that in rural districts, where life was simple and medieval, there was greater comfort and peace and less barbarity and coarseness, nevertheless, it is equally true that the scenes of English country life in the eighteenth century, that have come down to us in literature and painting, are more often conventional than real. Vested interests and the rights of property were deemed of greater importance than the rights of humanity, and society clung tenaciously to the old safeguards and defenses that checked the inrush of new ideas. There was a great absence of interest in technical invention and improvement. Because the landed classes were in the ascendant, agriculture was the only national interest receiving attention—drainage, rotation of crops, and the treatment of the soil being the only practical activities that attracted capital. The concerns and welfare of those without the right to vote were largely ignored; and it is no mere coincidence that the waste of human life, which was at its worst in London between 1720 and 1750, with the population of England declining during that period, should not have been checked until after 1780. The age was not one of progress in government, social organization, or humanitarianism; and it is important to note that the reconstruction of English manners and ways of living, and the movement leading to the diminution of crime, to sanitation, the greater abundance of food, and amelioration of living conditions—particularly in the towns and among the poorer classes—came after, and not before, the American Revolution.

The state of mind, to which were due the conditions thus described, permeated all phases of British life and government, and determined the attitude of the ruling classes toward the political, as well as the social, order. These classes were composed in a preponderant degree of landed proprietors, whose feelings of feudal superiority and tenacious adherence to the ideas and traditions of their class were determining factors in political life both in Parliament and the country. They believed that their institutions provided a sufficient panacea of all constitutional ills and could not imagine wherein these institutions needed serious revision. They were convinced that the existing system preserved men's liberties better than any that had gone before, and they wanted no experiments or dangerous leaps in the dark. They not only held as a tenet of faith that those who owned the land should wield political power, but they were certain that such an arrangement had the sanction of God. They revered the British system of government, its principles and philosophy, as the embodiment of human wisdom, grounded in righteousness and destined by nature to serve the purpose of man. They saw it admired abroad as the most enlightened government possessed by any nation in the world, and so credited it with their unprecedented prosperity and influence as a nation. They likened its critics to Milton's Lucifer, attacking "the sacred and immovable mount of the whole constitution", as a contemporary phrased it, and they guarded it as the Israelites guarded the ark of the covenant. Woe to him who would defile it!

Nor were they any less rigid in their attitude toward the colonies in America. Colonial policy had developed very slowly and did not take on systematic form until well on in the eighteenth century; but when once it became defined, the ruling classes regarded it in certain fundamental aspects—at least in official utterance—as fixed as was the constitution itself. At first England did not take her colonies seriously as assets of commercial importance, but when after 1704 naval stores were added to the tobacco and sugar of Virginia and the West Indies, and it was seen that these commodities enabled England to obtain a favorable balance of trade with European countries, the value of the plantations in British eyes increased enormously. However, it was not until after 1750, when a favorable balance of trade was reached with the colonies themselves, that the mercantilist deemed the situation entirely satisfactory; and from that time on for twenty years—epochal years in the history of England's relations with America—the mercantilist idea of the place that a colony should occupy in the British scheme of things became fixed and unalterable. Though the colonies were growing by leaps and bounds, the authorities in Great Britain retained unchanged the policy which had been adopted more than half a century before. They did not essentially alter the instructions to the Board of Trade in all the eighty-six years of its existence. They created no true colonial secretary, even in 1768, and no department of any kind at any time for the exclusive oversight of American affairs. They saw no necessity for adopting new methods of managing colonial trade, even though the colonial situation was constantly presenting new problems for solution. Manufacturing was undoubtedly more discouraged in 1770 than it had been in 1699, when the first restrictive act was passed; and the idea that the colonies by their very nature were ordained to occupy a position of commercial dependence to the advantage and profit of the mother country was never more firmly fixed in the British mind than just before our Revolution. In fact, that event altered in no essential particular the British conception of the status of a colony, for as late as 1823, Sir Charles Ellis, undoubtedly voicing the opinion of his day, could say in Parliament that the colonial system of England had not been established for the sake of the colonies, but for the encouragement of British trade and manufactures. Thus for more than a century England's idea of what a colony should be underwent no important alteration whatever.

Equally unchangeable was the British idea of how a colony should be governed. In the long list of commissions and instructions drawn up in England for the guidance of the royal governors in America, there is to be found, with one exception only, nothing that indicates any progressive advance in the spirit and method of administration from 1696 to 1782. Year after year, the same arrangements and phraseology appear, conforming to a common type, admitting, it is true, important modifications in matters of detail, but in principle undergoing at no time in eighty-six years serious revision or reconstruction. These documents were drawn up in Whitehall according to a fixed pattern; the governors and councils were allowed no discretion; the popular assemblies were confined within the narrow bounds of inelastic formulae, which repeated, time after time, the same injunctions and the same commands; while the crown reserved to itself the full right of interference in all matters that were construed as coming under its prerogative. These instructions represented the rigid eighteenth-century idea of how a colony should be retained in dependence on the mother country. And what was true of the instructions was true of other documents also that had to do with America. For instance, the lists of queries to the governors, the questionnaires to the commodore-governors of the Newfoundland fishery, and the whole routine business of the fishery itself had become a matter of form and precedent, as conventional and stereotyped as were the polite phrases of eighteenth-century social intercourse. Rarely was any attempt made to adapt these instructions to the needs of growing communities such as the colonies were showing themselves to be; and only with the Quebec instructions of 1775, issued after the passage of the Quebec Act and under the guidance of a colonial governor of unusual common-sense, was there any recognition of a new colonial situation. In this document, which appeared at the very end of our colonial period, do we find something of a break from the stiff and legalistic forms that were customary in the earlier royal instructions, some appreciation of the fact that the time was approaching when a colony should be treated with greater liberality and be allowed to have some part in saying how it should be administered.

Without going further with our analysis we can say that during the half-century preceding our Revolution English habits of thought and methods of administration and government, both at home and in the colonies, had reached a state of immobility. To all appearances the current of the national life had settled into a backwater, and as far as home affairs were concerned was seemingly becoming stagnant. At a time when Pitt was breaking France by land and sea, and men on waking were asking what new territories had been added during the night to the British dominions, occurrences at home were barren of adventure, either in society or politics. Ministers were not true statesmen; they had no policies, no future hopes, no spirit of advance, no gifts of foresight or prophecy. In all that concerned domestic interests, they were impervious to suggestions, even when phrased in the eloquence of Pitt and Burke. They wanted no change in existing conditions; their eyes were fixed on traditions and precedents rather than on the obligations and opportunities of the future. Their tenure of office was characterized by inactivity, a casual handling of situations they did not understand and could not control, and a willingness to let the ship of state drift for itself. As a modern critic has said, they were always turning in an unending circle, one out, one in, one in, one out, marking time and never going forward.

To a considerable extent the narrow point of view and rigidity of attitude exhibited by the men who held office at Whitehall or sat in Parliament at Westminster can be explained by the fact that at this time officials and members of Parliament were also territorial magnates, lords of manors, and country squires, who were influenced in their political life by ideas that governed their relations with their tenantry and the management of their landed estates. It is not necessary to think of them as bought by king or ministers and so bound and gagged against freedom of parliamentary action. In fact, they were bound and gagged already by devotion to their feudal privileges, their family prerogatives, and their pride of landed proprietorship. They viewed the colonies somewhat in the light of tenancies of the crown, and as they themselves lived on the rents from their estates, so they believed that the king and the kingdom should profit from the revenues and returns from America. The point of view was somewhat that of a later Duke of Newcastle, who when reproached for compelling his tenants to vote as he pleased said that he had a right to do as he liked with his own. This landed aristocracy reflected the eighteenth-century spirit. It was sonorous, conventional, and self-satisfied, and shameless of sparkle or humor. It clung to the laws of inheritance and property, fearful of anything that might in any way offend the shades of past generations. In its criticism of the manners of others it was insular and arrogant, and was mentally so impenetrable as never to understand why any one, even in the colonies, should wish things to be other than they were or refuse to accept the station of life to which by Providence he had been called.

A government, representative of a privileged social and political order that took existing conditions as a matter of course, setting nature at defiance and depending wholly on art, was bound sooner or later to come into conflict with a people, whose life in America was in closest touch with nature and characterized by growth and change and constant readjustments. In that country were groups of men, women, and children, the greater portion of whom were of English ancestry, numbering at first a few hundreds and eventually more than two millions, who were scattered over many miles of continent and island and were living under various forms of government. These people, more or less unconsciously, under the influence of new surroundings and imperative needs, were establishing a new order of society and laying the foundations of a new political system. The story of how this was done—how that which was English slowly and imperceptibly merged into that which was American—has never been adequately told; but it is a fascinating phase of history, more interesting and enlightening when studied against the English background than when construed as an American problem only. It is the story of the gradual elimination of those elements, feudal and proprietary, that were foreign to the normal life of a frontier land, and of the gradual adjustment of the colonists to the restraints and restrictions that were imposed upon them by the commercial policy of the mother country. It is the story also of the growth of the colonial assemblies and of the education and experience that the colonists were receiving in the art of political self-government. It is above all —and no phase of colonial history is of greater significance— the story of the gradual transformation of these assemblies from the provincial councils that the home government intended them to be into miniature parliaments. At the end of a long struggle with the prerogative and other forms of outside interference, they emerged powerful legislative bodies, as self-conscious in their way as the House of Commons in England was becoming during the same eventful years.

Here was an *impasse,* for the British view that a colonial assembly partook of the character of a provincial or municipal council was never actually true of any assembly in British America at any time in its history. From the beginning, each of these colonial bodies, in varying ways and under varying circumstances, assumed a position of leadership in its colony, and exercised, in a manner often as bewildering to the student of to-day as to an eighteenth-century royal governor, a great variety of executive, legislative, and judicial functions. Except in Connecticut and Rhode Island, requests for parliamentary privileges were made very early and were granted year after year by the governors—privileges that were essentially those of the English and Irish Houses of Commons and were consciously modelled after them. At times, the assemblies went beyond Parliament and made claims additional to the usual speaker's requests, claims first asked for as matters of favor but soon demanded as matters of right, as belonging to representative bodies and not acquired by royal gift or favor. One gets the impression that though the assemblies rarely failed to make the formal request, they did so with the intention of taking in any case what they asked for and anything more that they could secure. Gradually, with respect to privileges, they advanced to a position of amazing independence, freeing themselves step by step from the interfering power of the executive, that is, of the royal prerogative. They began to talk of these rights as ancient and inherent and necessary to the orderly existence of any representative body, and they became increasingly self-assertive and determined as the years passed.

Nor was this the only change affecting the assemblies to which the eighteenth-century Englishman was asked to adapt himself. The attitude of the assemblies in America found expression in the exercise of powers that had their origin in other sources than that of parliamentary privilege. They adopted rules of their own, that were sometimes even more severe than those of Parliament itself. They regulated membership, conduct, and procedure; ruled against drinking, smoking, and profanity, against unseemly, unnecessary, and tedious debate, against absence, tardiness, and other forms of evasion. They punished with great severity all infringement of rules and acts of contempt, and defended their right to do so against the governor and council on one side and the courts of the colony on the other. Nor did they even pretend to be consistent in their opposition to the royal prerogative, as expressed in the instructions to the royal governors, and in their manoeuvres they did not follow any uniform policy or plan. They conformed to these instructions willingly enough, whenever it was agreeable for them to do so; but if at any time they considered an instruction contrary to the best interest of a particular colony, they did not hesitate to oppose it directly or to nullify it by avoidance. In general, it may be said that they evaded or warded off or deliberately disobeyed such instructions as they did not like. Thus both consciously and unconsciously they were carving out a *lex parliamenti* of their own, which, evolving naturally from the necessity of meeting the demands of self-governing communities, carried them beyond the bounds of their own membership and made them responsible for the welfare of the colony at large.

The important point to remember is that the plan of governmental control as laid down in England was never in accord with the actual situation in America; that the Privy Council, the Secretary of State, and the Board of Trade seem not to have realized that their system of colonial administration was break-

ing down at every point. Their minds ran in a fixed groove
and they could construe the instances of colonial disobedience
and aggression, which they often noted, in no other terms than
those of persistent dereliction of duty. Either they did not see
or else refused to see the wide divergence that was taking place
between colonial administration as they planned it and colonial
administration as the colonists were working it out. Englishmen
saw in the American claims an attack upon an old, established,
and approved system. They interpreted the attitude of the
colonists as something radical and revolutionary, menacing
British prosperity, British political integrity, and the British
scheme of colonial government. Opposed by tradition and conviction to new experiments, even at home, they were unable to
sympathize with, or even to understand, the great experiment,
one of the greatest in the world's history, on trial across the sea.
There in America was evolving a new idea of sovereignty, inherent not in crown and Parliament but in the people of a
state, based on the principle—self-evident it may be to us to-day
but not to the Englishman of the eighteenth century—that
governments derive their just powers from the consent of the
governed. There was emerging a new idea of the franchise, as
a natural right, under certain conditions, of every adult citizen,
an idea which theoretically is not even yet accepted in Great
Britain. There was being established a new order of society,
without caste or privilege, free from economic restrictions and
social demarcations between class and class. There was taking
shape a new idea of a colony, a self-governing dominion, the
members of which were competent to develop along their own
lines, while working together with the mother country as part
of a common state.

For us to-day with our perspective it is easy to see the conflict approaching and some of us may think perhaps that the
British ministers and members of Parliament ought to have
realized that their own ideas and systems were fast outgrowing
their usefulness even for Great Britain herself; and that their
inflexible views of the colonial relationship were fast leading
to disaster. Yet we must keep in mind that it is always extraor-
dinarily difficult for a generation reared in the environment of

modern democracy to deal sympathetically with the English-man's point of view in the eighteenth century, or to understand why the ruling classes of that day so strenuously opposed the advance of liberalism both in England and America. The fact remains, however, that the privileged and governing classes in England saw none of these things. They were too close to events and too much a part of them to judge them dispassion-ately or to appreciate their real significance. These classes, within which we may well include the Loyalists in America, were possessed of inherited instincts, sentiments, and prejudices which they could no more change than they could have changed the color of their eyes or the texture of their skins. That which existed in government and society was to them a part of the fixed scheme of nature, and no more called for reconsideration than did the rising of the sun or the budding of the trees in spring. If Lord North had granted the claims of the colonists he probably would have been looked on by Parliament as hav-ing betrayed the constitution and impaired its stability, just as Peel was pilloried by a similar landowning Parliament in 1845, when he advocated the repeal of the corn laws. One has only to read the later debates on the subject of enclosures and the corn laws to understand the attitude of the British landowners toward the colonies from 1763 to 1776. To them in each instance it seemed as if the foundations of the universe were breaking up and the world in which they lived was sinking beneath their feet.

Primarily, the American Revolution was a political and con-stitutional movement and only secondarily one that was either financial, commercial, or social. At bottom the fundamental issue was the political independence of the colonies, and in the last analysis the conflict lay between the British Parliament and the colonial assemblies, each of which was probably more sensitive, self-conscious, and self-important than was the voting population that it represented. For many years these assemblies had fought the prerogative successfully and would have con-tinued to do so, eventually reducing it to a minimum, as the later self-governing dominions have done; but in the end it was Parliament, whose powers they disputed, that became the great antagonist. Canning saw the situation clearly when, half a century later, he spoke of the Revolution as having been a test of the equality of strength "between the legislature of this mighty kingdom . . . and the colonial assemblies", adding further that he had no intention of repeating in the case of Jamaica, the colony then under debate, the mistakes that had been made in 1776. Of the mistakes to which he referred the greatest was the employment of the deadly expedient of coercion, and he showed his greater wisdom when he determined, as he said, to keep back "within the penetralia of the constitution the transcendental powers of Parliament over a dependency of the British crown" and not "to produce it upon trifling occasions or in cases of petty refractoriness and temporary misconduct". How he would have met the revolution in America, based as it was on "the fundamental principles of political liberty", we cannot say; but we know that he had no sympathy with any attempt to force opinion back into paths that were outworn. That he would have foreseen the solution of a later date and have granted the colonies absolute and responsible self-government, recognizing the equality of the assemblies in domestic matters and giving them the same control over their home affairs as the people of Great Britain had over theirs, can be conjectured only by inference from his liberal attitude toward the South American republics. He stood half-way between the ministers of the Revolutionary period—blind, sensitive, and mentally unprogressive—and the statesmen of the middle of the nineteenth century, who were willing to follow the lead of those courageous and far-sighted Englishmen who saved the empire from a second catastrophe after 1830 and were the founders of the British colonial policy of to-day.

The revolt of the colonies from Great Britain began long before the battles of Moore's Creek Bridge and Lexington; before the time of James Otis and the writs of assistance; before the dispute over the appointment of judges in North Carolina and New York; before the eloquence of Patrick Henry was first heard in the land; and even before the quarrel in Virginia over the Dinwiddie pistole fee. These were but the outward and visible signs of an inward and factual divergence. The separation from the mother country began just as soon as the mercantile system of commercial control, the governmental system of colonial administration, and the whole doctrine of the inferior status of a colonial assembly began to give way before the pressure exerted and the disruptive power exercised by these young and growing colonial communities. New soil had produced new wants, new desires, new points of view, and the colonists were demanding the right to live their own lives in their own way. As we see it to-day the situation was a dramatic one. On one side was the immutable, stereotyped system of the mother country, based on precedent and tradition and designed to keep things comfortably as they were; on the other, a vital, dynamic organism, containing the seed of a great nation, its forces untried, still to be proved. It is inconceivable that a connection should have continued long between two such yokefellows, one static, the other dynamic, separated by an ocean and bound only by the ties of a legal relationship.

If my diagnosis is correct of the British state of mind in the eighteenth century, and the evidence in its favor seems overwhelming, then the colonists were as justified in their movement of revolt as were the Englishmen themselves in their movement for reform in the next century. Yet in reality no great progressive movement needs justification at our hands, for great causes justify themselves and time renders the decision. The revolt in America and the later reforms in Great Britain herself were directed against the same dominant ruling class that in their colonial relations as well as in their social and political arrangements at home preferred that the world in which they lived should remain as it was. Reform or revolt is bound to follow attempts of a privileged class to conduct affairs according to unchanging rules and formulae. The colonies had developed a constitutional organization equally complete with Britain's own and one that in principle was far in advance of the British system, and they were qualified to co-operate with the mother country on terms similar to those of a brotherhood of free nations such as the British world is becoming to-day. But England was unable to see this fact or unwilling to recognize it, and consequently America became the scene of a political unrest, which might have been controlled by compromise, but was turned to revolt by coercion. The situation is a very interesting one, for England is famous for her ability to compromise at critical moments in her history. For once at least she failed. In 1832 and later years, when she faced other great constitutional crises at home and in her colonies, she saved herself from revolution by understanding the situation and adjusting herself to it. Progress may be stemmed for a time, but it cannot be permanently stopped by force. A novelist has expressed the idea in saying: "You cannot fight and beat revolutions as you can fight and beat nations. You can kill a man, but you simply can't kill a rebel. For the proper rebel has an ideal of living, while your ideal is to kill him so that you may preserve yourself. And the reason why no revolution or religion has ever been beaten is that rebels die for something worth dying for, the future, but their enemies die only to preserve the past, and makers of history are always stronger than makers of empire." The American revolutionists had an ideal of living; it can hardly be said that in 1776 the Englishmen of the ruling classes were governed in their colonial relations by any ideals that were destined to be of service to the future of the human race.

6   *Oliver M. Dickerson*

"In this way the Navigation Acts became a cause of the Revolution, but not in the sense commonly presented"

Before his retirement in 1940 Oliver M. Dickerson had long taught history at Colorado State College. His most important work, The Navigation Acts and the American Revolution *(1951), was a full examination of England's commercial policy during the eighteenth century as it applied to the American colonies. Contrary to Bancroft, who had found the navigation acts to be an important cause of revolution, Dickerson discovered that they were a positive aid in binding the colonies to the mother country. Beginning in 1764, however, the British turned away from the encouragement of trade to a series of trade measures that contributed largely to the final break of the colonies with England.*

General statements in regard to the Navigation Acts are in need of extensive revision. As enacted in the seventeenth century and continued for more than a hundred years before the

SOURCE. Oliver M. Dickerson, *The Navigation Acts and the American Revolution.* Philadelphia: University of Pennsylvania Press, 1951, pp. 290–300. Copyright © 1951 by the University of Pennsylvania Press. Reprinted by permission of the publisher and the estate of Oliver M. Dickerson.

In this conclusion to his work Mr. Dickerson states that he may have offered his findings "somewhat dogmatically" in the belief that in preceding chapters he had provided ample proof.

outbreak of the Revolution, they were not, by 1763, the cause of serious irritation in America, nor were they made the basis of complaints on any considerable scale by the American leaders of the Revolution. The clause confining the carrying trade between the colonies and Great Britain to English ships and English seamen was as popular on this side of the water as on the other. It was specifically ratified by Virginia and Massachusetts and was never made the basis of a formal complaint during the entire century preceding the Revolution.

The clauses of the successive acts creating a list of enumerated products met with less opposition and more general support in America than has been supposed. The idea that enumeration was generally burdensome to the locality producing the commodity in question is not supported by the facts. Practically all of the enumerated products were grown in the West Indies or in the southern colonies. These were not the colonies that led in the revolt, with the exception of Virginia and South Carolina. In each case they had other grievances, and neither colony complained of the enumeration of tobacco, rice, and indigo as a grievance on the eve of the Revolution.

The enumeration clauses were apparently nowhere a cause of complaint, serious irritation, or widespread agitation, either for change in the laws or for separation from the mother country.

On the other hand, there is positive proof that enumeration was a real economic advantage to the regions where such articles were produced. Enumeration gave them an assured market for all that could be produced. Prices fluctuated, but even a low price at times was better than no price. Production of such articles acquired a stability that invited the investment of vast amounts of capital in labor, slaves, plantations, tools, shipping, warehouses, factors' establishments, and consumable supplies. Much of this capital was British and most of the debts due British creditors after the Revolution were in the areas where enumerated products were grown and by planters engaged in their production. Some of the active leaders of the Revolution in the southern states wrote off large fortunes in debts due to British creditors by the repudiation of these debts.

In addition enumeration made possible the creation of cen-

tralized markets in Britain with all of the mercantile facilities
to distribute the enumerated products to a world-wide market.
Communication was assured in time of war as well as peace
as a result of the great financial investments in Britain and
America, thus guaranteeing the arrival in the colonies of fleets
of ships to carry home the enumerated products at the right time
and to bring in the necessary supplies for the production of the
next crop.

These were real advantages not shared by the regions not
producing such products. Separation from the home country,
which ended enumeration, left all of the important enumerated
products in a declining condition. They became sick industries.
Rice and indigo never recovered their former world markets.
It was more than half a century before American tobacco interests could create for themselves the world-wide markets and
credit machinery they had enjoyed before the Revolution.

The clauses limiting American imports to British products
or to such European and Asiatic products as came from England
encountered some opposition and some evasion. This was
limited, however, in time and in products, and in no case was
the opposition coördinated and concerted. As time went on,
objection to this limitation upon the course of trade diminished,
and was practically nonexistent at the time of the Revolution.

The main reason for the steady acceptance of the routing of
foreign commodities through Great Britain was the elaborate
system of export bounties, export debentures, drawbacks, credits
extended by British merchants, and other facilities that made
England the most advantageous market in the world in which
the Americans could supply themselves with goods. Such advantages continued to increase up to the outbreak of the
Revolution and were a part of the whole complicated series of
trade acts. These advantages obviously were not objectionable
to the Americans.

Another phase of the trade acts was the definite encouragement of various local colonial industries by means of preferential
tariffs in England, strongly favoring the colonial product;
drawbacks of British duties for such portion of the product as
had to find a market in foreign countries; and direct parlia-

mentary bounties on colonial products, totaling millions of dollars and becoming more numerous in the years immediately preceding the Revolution. There are no American complaints on record against this practice. They strongly resemble the modern federal assistance to farmers in the United States.

The navigation and trade acts as a whole and considered as a part of a developed commercial policy had not resulted in widespread poverty or distress in any of the colonies. On the contrary all of the evidence shows that the continental colonies were generally prosperous, rapidly increasing in population, with every physical evidence of wealth more abundant than in England, and their wealth and prosperity boasted of by their own people and envied by their relatives in Britain. A constant stream of immigration from England, Scotland, and Ireland gave proof that colonial prosperity was well known in the home country. Finally, the rapidity with which the heavy colonial debts contracted during the French and Indian War were sunk demonstrated their fundamental prosperity as superior to that of Britain herself.

The limitations placed upon colonial manufactures were complained of by only a few Americans in New England and the middle colonies.

In general the objections to such limitations were confined to three articles—hats, woolen goods, and steel. The limitation on the first was in fact a limitation on the inter-colonial shipment of hats and in no case checked their actual manufacture. The prohibition against shipment from one colony to another applied as well to hats made in England as to those of local manufacture, and ultimately led to protests from English hat interests themselves. Much the same conditions applied to the regulation against wool and wool shipments. There never was a prosecution against American production of either woolen goods or steel.

Obviously manufacturing was too much in the household stage, the production of goods so largely for purely neighborhood consumption and those interested in the making of articles for export too limited in numbers and in geographic distribution to make paper restrictions a cause of the Revolution. No cases of actual enforcement occurred that are reported officially or in the newspapers of the period, which certainly aired every important cause of complaint.

Even Lord North admitted in the debates in Parliament in 1770 over the repeal of the main taxation program, that it was clearly not to the interest of Americans to engage in general manufacturing either for their own use or for export at this time.

On the other hand, the attempts of the Americans to develop manufactures of their own to take the place of the regular supplies from Great Britain, especially during the periods of aggressive nonimportation in 1765, 1767–1770, and 1733–75, created real alarm in England. British merchants, manufacturers, laborers, and shipowners feared that their vast business interests involved in the American trade were in danger. These fears led some of them to advocate and induced others to support the restrictive measures of Grenville, Townshend, and North that were ostensibly designed to preserve the old and profitable colonial markets. In this sense manufacturing in America became an important cause of the Revolution, not because Americans were oppressed and irritated by the trade acts limiting their manufacture, but because of the panicky reaction of men in England who were already engaged in manufacturing for general export and who feared the spectre of American competition which might permanently destroy their American market.

Evasion of the Navigation Acts was far less than has been assumed by many writers. There was probably no extensive evasion of the basic acts; and systematic smuggling in violation of the trade acts after the middle of the eighteenth century was limited mainly to two articles—tea and molasses. The repeal of the inland duties on tea in England, followed by the granting of drawbacks of the customs duties upon exportation to the colonies, removed most of the profits in the smuggling of tea and greatly diminished the practice. Lowering of the tax of six pence a gallon on foreign molasses to three pence and finally to a penny terminated any general illegal importation of molasses after 1766, and complaints on that section of the trade acts practically disappeared as a special issue. After 1766 there was no discrimination between British and foreign molasses, consequently that article was no longer under the trade laws.

The assumption that all shipowners and seamen violated the trade and navigation acts is without real foundation or tangible evidence. The smuggling charge was made against the Americans by some of the partisan Tories and was vehemently denied by leading revolutionary leaders.

The areas where illegal trading was, by common report, supposed to be most extensive were places where the Revolution received only lukewarm support or where the Tory population was very large, such as New York, Philadelphia, and Newport. Lawbreakers have never been famous for their patriotic following of lofty ideals. Even here the charges do not apply to the bringing in of foreign articles but to customed articles, largely British.

It is highly probable that as many, or even more, professional smugglers remained Tory as espoused the cause of the Revolution. Official evidence indicates that there may have been extensive smuggling from England in Virginia and Maryland where the great majority of the merchants were Tories. This is based upon the voluminous reports of Inspector General John Williams in 1769. He, however, was reporting in terms of the apparent evasion of the tax upon the importation of British manufactures without paying the duties. He indicates no suspicion that there was any general evasion of the trade acts by the importation of goods of foreign manufacture. There are many other reports by customs officers of presumed smuggling at other ports, but in every case they are referring to evasion of the revenue laws and not to violations of the trade and navigation acts.

There was organized opposition to the Sugar Act and the Townshend Revenue Act, especially in New England and the middle colonies. This was not due to the opposition of the Americans to the trade laws and had no possible relation to their attitude toward the old navigation and commercial system. This is shown by the letters, resolutions, and memorials of the Americans themselves.

Their opposition to the measures enacted after 1763 was not because they were trade regulations, *but because they were not laws of that kind.* They recognized these later acts as revenue laws, and hence a violation of the fundamental constitutional relationship that had been developing through the past century, under which all powers of taxation in the colonies belonged to their local assemblies. To the Americans the new program endangered their dearly won powers of self-government and threatened them with the loss of political liberty. Such laws also burdened British commerce instead of regulating it. This is not a mere assertion of American writers. The fullest statement of this attitude of Americans everywhere is in the formal unpublished reports made by the Customs Commissioners to the highest officials in England.

Failure to understand this fundamental issue as seen by the revolutionary leaders and by those who were attempting to enforce the revenue laws has led to a confusion of the resistance to the acts passed in the reign of George III with opposition to the general trade and navigation acts. The wholesale attempts to avoid paying the new duties have been falsely assumed to be a part of the general opposition to and evasion of the Navigation Acts.

The ministerial faction in England and some of their partisan adherents in America seized upon American opposition to the revenue measures to charge that the real objection of the Americans was to the trade and navigation acts. This charge was vehemently denied by leading Americans and their friends in England. At the time the accusation was made, it was generally recognized as unfair and put forward for partisan purposes.

There was an almost universal acceptance of the desirability of the trade regulations in both England and America as one of the essential foundations of British commercial and industrial prosperity. Besides, the American trade had been developed so long and so much capital was invested in it, so many British subjects made their living out of it, so many localities were so largely dependent upon the continuation of the old commercial relations, and so many millions of pounds had been loaned to American merchants and planters, that a charge that Americans were seeking to break down the complicated legal regulatory system upon which that trade was founded created real alarm. This fear gave the ministerial faction enough popular support for their ill-advised measures to enable them to stay in office and attempt to carry them out. Laws bitterly denounced in America as unconstitutional taxation measures and destructive of British commerce were defended in England as acts designed to restrain the Americans within the commercial system, and thus preserve the commercial relations upon which British prosperity had been built and a vast war debt contracted.

In this way the Navigation Acts became a cause of the Revolution, but not in the sense commonly presented. They were not the source of serious complaint by the Americans, but were used in England to justify and continue the measures after 1764 that were the object of American opposition and ultimately the cause of revolt. Such charges of American intentions stood in the way of effectual compromise as the issues approached the verge of civil war. The fear that concessions such as would satisfy the Americans would be only a prelude to a complete abrogation of the commercial system enabled the ministry to attempt to carry through its policy of asserting the authority of Parliament, by coercion if necessary.

The American leaders recognized this danger and tried in every way possible to convince the British public that they were not seeking to escape from the navigation system. This is shown in the resolutions of the Continental Congress, and in Franklin's specific offer to have the Navigation Acts reënacted by the colonial assemblies and even guaranteed for one hundred years, if the British would abandon their claims to parliamentary taxation.

Contemporary American and British historians understood the nature of the controversy so thoroughly that they did not include the Navigation Acts as one of the causes of the Revolution.

An examination of the contemporary literature on the eve of the Revolution leads to the conclusion that the trade and navigation system had built up in the course of a hundred years a self-sufficient commercial and political Empire that was the wonder of the world. The colonial sources of supply of raw materials, ship-building facilities, and loyal seamen made the British Empire potentially the most powerful nation in the world.

In the Seven Years War this loyal potential enabled Britain to sweep the seas clean of French and Spanish naval and commercial shipping, seize the French colonial empire with its added potential, and some of the richest prizes of the Spanish colonial empire. In 1763 the British Empire was in much the same relative world position as was the United States in 1945.

This vast commercial and colonial Empire was disintegrated and dissolved in ten years by a policy that undertook to substitute trade taxation for trade protection and encouragement. The cement of fair and relatively equal treatment in matters of commerce was dissolved by what happened in a few years of customs racketeering. This included the exploitation of American commerce by a new race of customs officers who sought to operate the customs service for their own personal profits. The bonding provisions of the new revenue laws were used to give legal color to the seizure of vessels on the most technical grounds. Excessive fees were exacted. New and unheard of burdens were imposed upon the coasting trade. Strictly local trade within individual provinces was forced to enter, clear, give bonds, carry cockets, etc., in spite of the rulings of the highest legal advisers of the crown. Informers, spies, stoolpigeons, and swarms of other officers, all supported out of the proceeds of the American revenue, or from fees and seizures for borderline causes, were created. The ancient rights of seamen to engage in little ventures of their own were made the basis of new prosecutions against their employers and seizure of their own little stocks of capital.

The new Board of Customs Commissioners devoted its energies to waging war upon ships, seamen, merchants, and commerce in the interest of revenue; multiplying officers and employees for this purpose; inaugurating a new and rapacious coast guard service manned by unprincipled individuals interested chiefly in personal plunder. This new coast guard service behaved like pirates and was soon at open war with the formerly loyal

American seamen. The officers of the navy were made customs officers and assigned to the same task of plundering American commerce for their own personal gain under the name of enforcing the new revenue regulations. The Union Jack on a British vessel had formerly stood for the protection of British commerce. Now its appearance aroused feelings like that of the old Jolly Roger.

From the beginning the Customs Commissioners were obsessed with the idea that the Americans were rebellious and the Commissioners needed military and naval power to enforce their decisions. Englishmen do not yield readily to coercion, and especially resent the threat of force. Formerly loyal, the Americans planned open and passive resistance to measures they considered illegal exercises of authority by placemen of a "wicked ministry."

The efforts of the Commissioners to use the revenue laws as a cloak to set up in America a centralized authority over domestic and foreign commerce through the extended use of admiralty courts; multiplication of writs of assistance: power to compel attorneys-general, colonial supreme courts, and even governors to do their bidding; and directed prosecution of suits for enormous sums against wealthy merchants who dared organize political opposition to their exactions, created in three short years a hostility toward customs officers from Quebec to the Caribbean hitherto unknown in British colonial relations.

None of the new exactions and demands for the exercise of arbitrary authority had any relation to the trade and navigation laws. They were thoroughly anti-trade. Americans said so in season and out of season. The majority of British merchants and manufacturers interested in the colonial trade agreed with the Americans and agitated for a repeal of the anti-trade legislation. Finally in 1770 even the King's Friends conceded that taxation of British manufactures going to colonial markets was contrary to sound trade principles and moved for the repeal of all the new taxes except that on tea.

This was retained because it was a real source of revenue for support of the numerous placemen which the King's Friends in England needed to keep themselves in office. It was the only fund out of which colonial officials could be paid. While the concessions were a great relief to the Americans, they were inadequate. The customs service was still administered for revenue and not for trade purposes. Three years of gross mistreatment at the hands of a plundering revenue service had created in important places a deep sense of resentment. The old sentiment of loyalty was gone.

A century of wisely administered trade and navigation laws had developed the greatest and most loyal colonial Empire in the world. Abandonment of that policy destroyed that Empire in less than ten years. The former cement of favored trade relations that bound colonies and home country together had been dissolved. The new policy of taxation and exploitation of America in the interests of a political faction in England was a disintegrating force that destroyed loyalty. The degree of damage was different in different areas, depending upon the way the revenue acts were administered. In some areas they were so administered as to produce very little hostility. In general these were the areas where there was little concentration of the import trade from England or from the West Indies. The heavy taxation, the excessive fees, and the seizures were concentrated in a few trading colonies. These were the centers of the revolutionary movement. The areas where the old trade and navigation laws operated relatively undisturbed by the new taxation program remained loyal.

7

Arthur M. Schlesinger

"The merchants found themselves instinctively siding with the home government"

During the first third and more of the twentieth century Arthur M. Schlesinger was one of a large group of historians who sought to dis-cover what was revolutionary about the American Revolution or, to phrase it differently, what the Revolution was other than a movement for political independence from England. Mr. Schlesinger's approach to the problem constituted an in-depth study of the American merchants throughout the colonies in the expectation that an understanding of their economic interests and political activities would go far toward revealing the well-springs of the revolutionary movement. As the fol-lowing passage shows, he discovered an interesting interplay between the upper-class merchants and the political radicals.

The enactment of the coercive acts by Parliament called forth the union of interests and action in America, which the opposition to the East India Company in the leading seaports had failed to evoke. The chief of these laws were intended to deal with the lawless conditions which had arisen in the province

SOURCE. Arthur Meier Schlesinger, *The Colonial Merchants and the Amer-ican Revolution, 1763–1776,* Vol. LXXVIII of Columbia University Studies in History, Economics and Public Law. New York: Columbia University Press. 1918, pp. 305–309. Reprinted by permission of the publisher.

of Massachusetts Bay out of the tea commotions. The first of
the series, the Boston Port Act, received the royal assent on the
last day of March, 1774. This act provided for the closing of
the harbor of Boston to commerce from and after June 1 and
the transfer of the custom house to Marblehead and the capital
to Salem. The port of Boston was to be re-opened when the
East India Company and the customs officers and others had
been reimbursed for the losses sustained by them during the
riots, and when the king in privy council was satisfied that
trade might be safely carried on there and the customs duly
collected.

After an interval of two months, two other acts were passed
which provided for thorough-going alterations of the constitution of the province. The governor's council, which, being
elective by the Assembly, had hitherto obstructed all efforts to
suppress rioting, was now made appointive by the king, as in
all other royal provinces. A direct blow was aimed at the system
of committees of correspondence by the provision placing town
meetings under the immediate control of the governor from
and after August 1, and permitting only the annual meeting
for the election of officers to be held without his express
authorization. The way was prepared for a rigorous execution
of the customs laws by providing that a person might be tried
in another province or in Great Britain, who was charged with
a capital crime committed "either in the execution of his duty
as a magistrate, for the suppression of riots or in the support
of the laws of revenue, or in acting in his duty as an officer of
revenue," or as acting in a subordinate capacity in either case.
The three acts passed with great majorities. A motion to re-
scind the tea duty called forth a remarkable speech in favor of
repeal by Edmund Burke; but the motion was lost by a large
vote.

The receipt of the news of the Boston Port Act put a new face
on public affairs in America. It changed completely the nature
of the contest with Parliament which had been going on in-
termittently since 1764. It created the basis for a realignment
of forces and strength, the importance of which was to be a
fundamental factor in the later development of events. Hitherto

the struggle with Parliament had been, in large part, inspired and guided by the demand of the mercantile class for trade reforms. Each new act of Parliament had accentuated or ameliorated business distress in the colonies; and in proportion to the remedial character of the legislation, the barometer of American discontent had risen or fallen. To carry on their propaganda successfully, the merchants had found it necessary to form alliances with their natural enemies in society—with the intelligent, hopeful radicals who dreamed of a semi-independent American nation or something better, and with the innumerable and nameless individuals whose brains were in their biceps, men who were useful as long as they could be held in leash. The passage of the Boston Port Act and the other laws brought things to an issue between these two elements, already grown suspicious of each other. The question in controversy between Parliament and the colonies was changed in an instant from a difference over trade reforms to a political dispute, pure and simple, over the right of Parliament to punish and prevent mob violence through blockading Boston and expurgating the Massachusetts constitution.

In this new aspect of the controversy the merchants found themselves instinctively siding with the home government. No commercial principle was at stake in the coercive acts; and the Boston violence was a manifestation of mob rule which every self-respecting merchant abhorred from his very soul. Nor could he see any commercial advantage which might accrue from pursuing the will-o'-the-wisp ideas of the radicals. The uncertain prospect which the radical plans held forth was not comparable with the tangible benefits which came from membership in the British empire under existing conditions; even absolute freedom of trade meant little in view of the restrictive trade systems of the leading nations of the world, the comparative ease with which the most objectionable parliamentary regulations continued to be evaded, and the insecure, if not dangerous, character of any independent government which the radicals might establish. When all was said and done, the merchants knew that their welfare depended upon their connection with Great Britain —upon the protection afforded by the British navy, upon the acquisition of new markets by British arms, upon legislation which fostered their shipping, subsidized certain industries and protected the merchants from foreign competition in British markets. Many details of this legislation had proved defective, but Parliament had shown a disposition to correct the worst features; and this disposition would, in all probability, continue, since British capital invested in American trade had a powerful representation in Parliament.

From the time of the passage of the coercive acts by Parliament, thus, there became evident a strong drift on the part of the colonial mercantile class to the British viewpoint of the questions at issue. Many merchants at once took their stand with the forces of government and law and order; these men may properly be classed as conservatives, or loyalists, in the same sense that the royal official class were. Others believed that all was not yet lost and that, by remaining in the movement, they could restrain its excesses and give it a distinctly conservative cast. Such men were, for the time being at least, moderates, being willing, though for partisan reasons, to indulge in extra-legal activities.

But the coercive acts were equally important in making converts to the radical position. Whereas the mob destruction of the tea had antagonized many people, the enactment of the severe punitive acts served, in the judgment of many of them, to place the greater guilt on the other side.

8   *Frederick B. Tolles*
"The 'Jameson thesis' is still sound, and,
what is more important, still vital and suggestive"

Frederick B. Tolles, Jenkins Professor of Quaker History at Swarth-more College, is the author of various works on Pennsylvania history which include Meeting House and Counting House: The Quaker Merchants of Colonial Philadelphia, 1682–1763 (1948). *In 1954 Mr. Tolles chose to write a commentary on a small but important book by J. Franklin Jameson,* The American Revolution Considered as a Social Movement, *which had been published in 1925. Mr. Tolles' article necessarily refers frequently to the research of others and provides, in effect, not only a resume of the main points that Jameson had made in his work but an indication of the erosion and modification that had occurred to the Jameson thesis during the intervening time.*

Sometimes a single essay, a monograph, or a series of lectures makes historiographical history. It was so in 1893 when Frederick Jackson Turner read his paper on "The Significance of the Frontier in American History." It was so again in 1913 when Charles A. Beard published his *Economic Interpretation of the Constitution*. And it was so in 1925 when J. Franklin Jameson

SOURCE. Frederick B. Tolles, "The American Revolution Considered as a Social Movement: A Re-Evaluation," *American Historical Review*, **60** (October 1954), 1–12. Reprinted by permission of the author.

delivered his four lectures at Princeton on "The American Revolution Considered as a Social Movement."

At first glance the comparison with Turner and Beard may seem strained. We are accustomed to think of Jameson as a scholar's scholar, a kind of indispensable historical midwife—curator and editor of manuscripts, director of other men's research, editor of the *American Historical Review*—not as a pathbreaker, an innovator. But this is to do him less than justice. *The American Revolution Considered as a Social Movement* stands as a landmark in recent American historiography, a slender but unmistakable signpost, pointing a new direction for historical research and interpretation. Before Jameson, the American Revolution had been a chapter in political, diplomatic, and military history, a story of Faneuil Hall and Lexington, Independence Hall and Valley Forge, Versailles and Yorktown. After Jameson, it became something different, something greater—a seismic disturbance in American society, a sudden quickening in the American mind.

The American Revolution, like the French, Jameson believed, was accompanied by social and cultural changes of profound significance:

"The stream of revolution, once started, could not be confined within narrow banks, but spread abroad upon the land. Many economic desires, many social aspirations were set free by the political struggle, many aspects of colonial society profoundly altered by the forces thus let loose. The relations of social classes to each other, the institution of slavery, the system of landholding, the course of business, the forms and spirit of the intellectual and religious life, all felt the transforming hand of revolution, all emerged from under it in shapes advanced many degrees nearer to those we know."

No more than Turner's or Beard's was Jameson's notion wholly new. Just a year earlier, in his massive volume on *The American States during and after the Revolution*, Allan Nevins had devoted fifty pages to the task of demonstrating in impressive detail that "a social and intellectual revolution" occurred between Lexington and Yorktown. Nearly twenty years before Carl Becker had described the Revolution as a twofold contest: for home-rule on the one hand, for "the democratization of American politics and society" on the other. As far back as 1787 Benjamin Rush had perceived that the American revolution was bigger than the American war, that the real revolution was in "the principles, morals, and manners of our citizens," and that, far from being over, that revolution had only begun.

Jameson's view of the Revolution was not new, but no one hitherto had marshaled the evidence so compactly, conveyed it so lucidly, or argued from it so persuasively. Perceptive historians immediately greeted his little volume as a gem of historical writing—"a truly notable book," Charles A. Beard called it, "... cut with a diamond point to a finish, studded with novel illustrative materials, gleaming with new illumination, serenely engaging in style, and sparingly garnished with genial humor."

The influence of this little book with the long title has grown steadily. A year after its publication, the Beards summarized its thesis in their widely read *Rise of American Civilization*. Jameson's emphasis on social factors harmonized perfectly with the intellectual and political climate of the 1930's. In 1940, after the author's death, a second edition appeared, and in 1950 a third—an unusual tribute to a set of academic lectures. With the passage of a quarter-century, the book has achieved the standing of a minor classic. One will find hardly a textbook that does not paraphrase or quote Jameson's words, borrow his illustrations, cite him in its bibliography. The notion of the Revolution as a social upheaval has achieved the final seal of acceptance: it has been taken over by the historical novelists —by such writers as Kenneth Roberts and Howard Fast, to name two rather unlikely bedfellows.

Jameson, one suspects, had no idea he was writing a classic. His aim was simply to challenge American historians by opening new windows on the Revolutionary era, suggesting new directions for future research, throwing out tentative hypotheses for others to test. Over the past quarter-century historians have risen to his challenge with a flood of articles, monographs,

academic dissertations, and full-dress histories bearing on one
or another of his propositions. But the average textbook-writer,
one is tempted to believe, has not got beyond Jameson. The
time has come to go back and ask how Jameson's original thesis
stands up in the light of all this detailed research; what modifications, if any, must be made; what further extensions, if any,
are possible.

Jameson disposed his arguments under four rubrics—the
status of persons, the land, industry and commerce, thought and
feeling. If we recognize, as he did, that such divisions are
purely arbitrary, we may adopt his procedure.

American society, he suggested, was measurably democratized
during the Revolution. The upper stratum, the old colonial
aristocracy, was largely liquidated—by banishment, voluntary
exile, or impoverishment. New groups rose to the surface to
take their places. "In most states the strength of the revolutionary
party lay most largely in the plain people," and the social
changes which they brought about naturally tended "in the
direction of levelling democracy." Broadening of the suffrage
elevated "whole classes of people . . . in their social status,"
and the revolutionary philosophy of liberty wrought improvements in the condition of the most debased class in America—
the Negro slaves.

Recent studies of individual states and regions seem to suggest
that Jameson was too sweeping when he equated colonial aristo-
crats with Loyalists and implied that this group was erased
from American society. In eastern Massachusetts it was perhaps
true that "a majority of the old aristocracy" emigrated. But in
the central and western part of the state the oldest, most respected families chose the Whig side and remained to perpetuate
their local rule in the days of the early Republic. In New
Hampshire, except around Portsmouth, society had never been
highly stratified, and the Tory emigration bore away few out-
standing individuals. In Connecticut, where "the native aristocracy of culture, wealth, religion, and politics" tended to be
loyal to the crown, at least half of the Tories never left the state.
Others were welcomed back even before the war was over.

Within six months of the peace treaty, New Haven was openly
extending an invitation to former Loyalists to return, and
President Ezra Stiles of Yale College was grumbling about efforts
"silently to bring the Tories into an Equality and Supremacy
among the Whigs." In New York and Philadelphia, many prom-
inent merchants—perhaps the majority—were Loyalists, or at
least "neutralists," and they stayed on in such numbers as to
give a definite tone to postwar society, politics, and business in
these important centers. In Maryland, the "internal" Revolution
turns out to have been a struggle between one group of aristo-
crats—planters, merchants, lawyers—and another; the "plain
people" took little part in the conflict and the resultant social
shifts were minimal. In Virginia, of course, most of the "F.F.V.'s"
were Whigs, and their control of politics was to continue through
the days of the "Virginia dynasty." In the North Carolina back
country it was the "plain people"—the old Regulators—who were
most stubbornly Loyalist. Clearly Jameson's generalizations about
the fate of the old aristocracy must be qualified.

What about the new democracy of the Revolutionary period?
Unquestionably a sense of dignity and importance came to the
common man—the small farmer, the town artisan—as a result
of his revolutionary activities and the limited extension of the
suffrage. But before we can say with assurance how democratic
the new society was, we must answer the prior question: how
undemocratic was the old? No one will dispute the fact that
provincial society was stratified, that class distinctions existed,
that political and social equality were hardly dreamed of. A
recent brilliant study of electoral practices in colonial Massachusetts raises, however, some questions. By means of ingenious
statistical methods and samplings of contemporary opinion, the
author of this study has shown rather convincingly that, in the
Bay Colony at least, practically all adult males had the vote.
Massachusetts society before 1776, he concludes, was "very close
to a complete democracy." And he hints of further revisions to
come. "As for the 'internal revolution' in other colonies," he
says, "—perhaps we should take another look. There is more
than a hint in the records that what applies to Massachusetts

applies without too much change to other colonies as well."

Though the Negro slave received some indirect benefits from the Revolution, the indentured servant, Jameson found, received none. Nor has subsequent research uncovered any important evidence that he overlooked. While he was dwelling on the negative side, Jameson might have mentioned another large dependent class that gained nothing in status as a result of the Revolution. Even before independence was declared, that doughty feminist Abigail Adams was writing to her husband in Congress: "By the way, in the new code of laws which I suppose it will be necessary for you to make, I desire you would remember the ladies and be more generous and favorable to them than your ancestors." Her husband wrote back, as much in earnest as in jest: "Depend on it, we know better than to repeal our masculine systems." It was to be nearly three quarters of a century before the Declaration of Independenc would be revised by a group of determined ladies at Seneca Falls to read: "All men and women are created equal." Both negative and positive evidence, then, suggests that the Revolution made less difference in the status of persons in America than Jameson believed.

The doctrine that underlies Jameson's second lecture is, quite explicitly, economic determinism: "political democracy," he says flatly, "came to the United States as a result of economic democracy." The movement for manhood suffrage which reached its fruition in Jacksonian America, he maintains, was rooted in a peculiarly American type of land tenure—the system of small holdings or what he chooses to call "peasant proprietorship." This system the Revolution fixed upon the nation when it swept away the royal restrictions, the archaic manorial laws and usages which had encumbered the land throughout the colonial period. There was, he makes clear, "no violent outbreak," no bloodly massacre of landlords as in France a decade later. Still, "in a quiet, sober, Anglo-Saxon way a great change was effected in the land-system of America between the years 1775 and 1795." Specifically, the changes were of three sorts: the discontinuance of quitrents and of the king's right to mast-trees, the abolition of primogeniture and entail, the confiscation and distribution of the Tory estates.

The importance of the quitrents and the king's "broad arrow" was probably more symbolic than real. Jameson himself admitted this: payment of quitrents, he pointed out, was "largely evaded"; the law giving the king's surveyors the right to reserve the tallest, straightest pine trees for the Royal Navy "was not rigorously enforced." Still, no historian will deny the importance of an emotion-laden symbol, and Jameson insists, quite rightly, that the quitrent and the king's "broad arrow" were symbols of an obsolete and alien feudalism, that until they were done away with, private property was not private property.

There is high authority, of course, for attaching great significance to the abolition of primogeniture and entail in Virginia—the authority of Thomas Jefferson. But these gestures too, it now appears, were more important in the realm of symbol than of economic reality. In point of fact, neither primogeniture nor entail operated to any important degree in Virginia. Recent research has shown that most estates in the Old Dominion were not entailed but could be freely alienated. And primogeniture was mandatory only if the property owner died intestate. Most Virginia planters were careful to make wills. By their wills they often distributed their property among all their sons, and sometimes even their daughters. So Jefferson, in the words of his most authoritative biographer, "did not destroy the country gentry as a group with the blows of his mighty ax, and there is insufficient reason to believe that he wanted to." What he did was merely to "remove legal vestiges of Old World aristocracy." The sweeping conclusion reached by a recent student of this problem in Virginia may well apply to other colonies: "No radical change of custom in devising estates resulted from the abolition of primogeniture and entail."

On the confiscation of Loyalist lands much has been written of late years. The evidence has not been canvassed for all the states, but a definite conclusion seems to be emerging: that considerably less diffusion and democratization of landownership resulted from the breakup of these estates and their disposition in small parcels than Jameson supposed.

The most intensive study has been centered on the southern counties of New York, where the DeLanceys, the Bayards, the

Philipses held sway in colonial times over their vast baronies. When the revolutionary New York government seized the estates and sold them off, some of the land, to be sure, went to former tenants and other landless individuals. But the bulk of it was bought up by wealthy patriots and merely augmented the domains of rival families like the Livingstons, Schuylers, and Roosevelts. "While it is true," concludes the author of this study, "that the disposal of the loyalist estates effected a greater diffusion of ownership, it is questionable whether it went far toward a radical redistribution of landed wealth and a new social and economic order."

The same thing seems to have been true in Maryland, where wealthy Whig planters and speculators bought up a large proportion of the desirable Tory lands in Baltimore and Frederick counties. Nor is the story greatly different in western Massachusetts or New Hampshire. The South Carolina confiscation laws, in the opinion of a contemporary, was actually "so framed that a man who wants land has no chance to get any," for the state required security which only the wealthy landowner could provide.

The case of North Carolina is instructive. The authority on the Loyalists of that state, noting that the confiscated lands were sold in plots averaging two hundred acres, concludes with Jameson that the confiscations "tended to make the Revolution economic and social as well as political." From his own evidence, however, one could draw the equally justified inference that many a wealthy patriot took advantage of the bargain prices to increase his holdings and consequently his social status. The largest Tory estate was that of the great speculator Henry McCulloh—some 40,000 acres. Of the ninety purchasers of McCulloh's lands thirty-four bought more than one tract. Some acquired as many as ten or fifteen, thereby creating estates as large as 5,000 acres. Robert Raiford purchased parcels from five different Tories and put together an estate of more than a thousand acres. The 3,600-acre estate of Thomas Hooper passed almost intact to John McKinsey. Before a final generalization can be made about the social effects of the confiscations in North Carolina, we need to know more about the previous economic status of the purchasers.

The largest estate to be confiscated in America, as Jameson pointed out, was that of the Penn family. By the Divesting Act of 1779 the Pennsylvania legislature assumed control of twenty-one and a half million acres—all the ungranted lands which by royal charter had belonged to the proprietors. But this proprietary land, from which the Penns had never received any income, was comparable, surely, to the ungranted crown lands which fell into the hands of the other commonwealths. Much more significant is the fact that the private manors, the "proprietary tenths," of the Penns, amounting to more than 500,000 acres, together with the quitrents on them, were specificially "confirmed, ratified and established for ever" in the hands of the Penn family—and this by the most "radical" of all the revolutionary legislatures!

Clearly, there are two ways of reading the evidence concerning the confiscation and sale of Loyalist lands. Jameson, who was arguing a thesis, chose to stress the "democratizing" effects. But there were other social consequences of an opposite tendency —the aggrandizement of certain individuals and families already well entrenched, the opportunities opened for speculation—and we shall not understand all the social results of this great sequestration of lands until we assess these as well.

In particular, until someone has studied the social effects of land speculation in the Revolutionary and post-Revolutionary era as Professor Paul W. Gates has done for a later period, we shall not know whether the operations of the speculators hastened or delayed settlement, encouraged or hindered the system of small holdings. Meanwhile, we may note that Professor Abernethy considers the Virginia land office act of 1779 (drafted, incidentally, by Thomas Jefferson) "a colossal mistake," a blow to economic democracy, and a retarding influence on settlement because it played into the hands of speculators and thus *prevented* the diffusion of land in small holdings. By this act, he says, "democracy was defeated in Virginia at the moment when it might have had its birth."

Land speculation was, of course, a form of business enterprise. And business enterprise, it is now clear, took a sharp spurt as a direct result of Revolutionary conditions. That Jameson should have perceived and stressed this in 1925 is sufficiently remarkable. His chapter on "Industry and Commerce" undoubtedly opened the eyes of many American historians to the economic facts which, as everyone now recognizes, are as crucial in the history of a war as the political, diplomatic, and military facts.

Some of the new economic paths which the Revolution opened, turned out to be blind alleys. Postwar interest in the improvement of agriculture, reflected in the sudden popularity of farmers' societies, proved to be short-lived and relatively ineffectual. In some regions the wartime growth of manufacturing, which Jameson noted, was choked off by the postwar flood of cheap British goods, which he neglected to mention.

But in other ways enterprise burgeoned and flourished under wartime and postwar conditions. Opportunities for quick gains in privateering and profiteering, the opening of new markets, the expansion of the credit system, the injection of new supplies of specie into the economy as a result of foreign borrowing, the rise of new business groups around men like Jeremiah Wadsworth, William Duer, Robert Morris, the very idea (a new one for Americans) of large-scale business association—all these were constructive economic forces generated by the Revolution. Especially important were the rise of banking and the spread of incorporation. In the words of one economic historian, the Bank of North America, which opened in Philadelphia in 1782, "was identified with the American Revolutionary 'settlement,'—as the Bank of England was with that of the 'Glorious Revolution.' "

The same scholar gives us some revealing statistics on the chartering of business corporations: "In contrast with the half-dozen American business charters granted in the entire colonial period, eleven were issued in the United States between 1781 and 1785, twenty-two between 1786 and 1790, and 114 between 1791 and 1795." Economic facts of this order have led one writer to treat the American Revolution as "the triumph of American mercantile capitalism." Whether or not one wishes to adopt this view, it is clear, as Jameson dimly perceived, that the Revolution loosed potent new forces in the American

economy. How these forces were related to the social and political democracy which Jameson saw as products of the Revolution
remains to be studied.

When he turned from the hard facts of economic history to
the impalpable realm of "thought and feeling," Jameson was
less at home. Yet even here he opened vistas which a generation
of intellectual and cultural historians have explored with profit.
The greater part of his final lecture is concerned with the effect
of independence on the churches—with disestablishment and the
separation of church and state, with the reorganization of the
churches on a national basis, with the wartime decline of
religious life and the postwar spread of liberal theologies. Subsequent research has added little to Jameson's account of these
matters, except to fill in details. What Jameson did—and it
was no trifling achievement—was to bring American church
history within the purview of American historians—to take, as
it were, the first steps toward giving this neglected orphan child
a home and a standing within the family of historical disciplines.

Certain of his insights, naturally, have proved more fruitful
than others. His *obiter dictum* to the effect that military men
can never again play the part in public life that they played
after the Revolution falls strangely on our ears, who have known
the proconsulate of MacArthur, the foreign ministry of Marshall,
the Presidency of Eisenhower. Curiously, Jameson found little
evidence of educational advance in the Revolutionary era, except
for the founding of new colleges. Had he taken a broader view
of education, he might have recognized a number of important
developments directly or indirectly related to wartime experience: the improvement of medicine (including dentistry)
and of medical education; the emergence of civil engineering
from military engineering; the founding of Judge Tapping
Reeve's "law school" at Litchfield, Connecticut, in 1784; the
diffusion of scientific knowledge through the revived activity
of the American Philosophical Society and the founding of the
American Academy of Arts and Sciences; the popularity of
pamphleteering as a form of mass education; and—not least
important—the informal education, the widening of horizons,
that resulted from wartime mobility, from the fact that, for the

first time, many Americans rubbed elbows—and minds—not only with Europeans but with other Americans. The school of intellectual and cultural historians which has sprung up in the last quarter century has made much of the "intellectual democracy" and the "cultural nationalism" which Jameson vaguely perceived as concomitants, in the realm of "thought and feeling," of the American Revolution.

The danger here as elsewhere is that the historian, misled by his enthusiasm for the concept of "revolution," will posit too abrupt a set of changes, will pay too little attention to the evidences of historical continuity. Jameson himself did not altogether avoid this pitfall. For example, he wrote that "Joel Barlow's *Vision of Columbus,* or President Stiles's celebrated election sermon on *The United States Elevated to Glory and Honor,* could not possibly have been written twenty years earlier." If he meant by this that the idea of the United States as an independent nation was not entertained in the 1760's, the statement is obviously correct, though hardly startling. If he meant that before 1775 no American felt or expressed love for the land, pride in its people, confidence in its future, he was just as obviously wrong. For one finds strong feelings of American patriotism in a pre-Revolutionary poem like Freneau and Brackenridge's "The Rising Glory of America," written in 1771, in the sermons of Samuel Davies and Jonathan Mayhew in the 1750's, even in Judge Samuel Sewall's proud paean to his beloved Plum Island, Crane Pond, and Turkey Hill as far back as the last decade of the seventeenth century. Indeed the points at which the supports of Jameson's thesis seem weakest—where for example he argues for sharper changes in the political and social status of individuals than can be justified on the evidence —are precisely those points at which he overlooked or underestimated dynamic forces already present in the society of late colonial America.

Still, a historian who fashions so useful a conceptual tool, who popularizes so fruitful a hypothesis, who enlarges so notably our understanding of a significant era in American history, can be forgiven a few oversights, a few overstatements. Basically, the "Jameson thesis" is still sound, and, what is more important, still vital and suggestive, capable of still further life, still greater usefulness. Jameson, after all, did much more than give us a new approach to the American Revolution. He formulated and cogently applied to a particular period an important general thesis—"the thesis that all the varied activities of men in the same country and period have intimate relations with each other, and that one cannot obtain a satisfactory view of any one of them by considering it apart from the others." For this he deserves homage as one of the founders of American social and cultural history.

9

Robert E. Brown
In Massachusetts "we find . . . a revolution
to preserve a social order rather than to change it"

In 1955, in a study of Massachusetts from 1691 to 1780, Robert E.
Brown sharply attacked the socio-economic historians. This school, he
argued, had used two assumptions to label as undemocratic the society
that produced the American Revolution: first, the franchise had been
severely restricted, and, second, the older, aristocratic seacoast areas had
possessed an unfairly large representation at the expense of the more
recently settled interior regions. These same historians, Brown con-
tinued, usually then described an American Revolution that represented
a victory of the common man over the ruling class.

Using Massachusetts to test this interpretation, Brown found instead a
middle-class society with property widely distributed, a fluid economic
structure, and an extensive franchise—all conditions that obviated the
need of an upper-class—lower-class struggle for economic and political
superiority.

In Massachusetts . . . we find one of the unique "revolutions"
in world history—a revolution to preserve a social order rather
than to change it. It was not, as we have often assumed, a dual

[1] Robert E. Brown, *Middle-Class Democracy and the Revolution in Massa-chusetts, 1691–1780.* Ithaca, N. Y.: Cornell University Press, 1955, pp. 401–404, 405–406. Copyright © 1955 by the American Historical Association. Re-printed by permission of the American Historical Association and the author.

revolution in which Americans won their independence from the British on one hand, and in which unenfranchised and underprivileged lower classes wrested democratic rights from a privileged local aristocracy on the other.

To understand what happened, we must first have a clear picture of Massachusetts society. Economically speaking, it was a middle-class society in which property was easily acquired and in which a large portion of the people were property-owning farmers. There was undoubtedly more economic democracy for the common man then than there is now. A large permanent labor class was practically nonexistent; men could either acquire land and become farmers or work for themselves as skilled artisans. If we insist that Americans who came to this country brought their accustomed class or caste lines with them, we must do so in the face of all the evidence to the contrary. If there was anything that observers at the time agreed on, it was that American society was almost the exact opposite of European society. There was nothing approaching the spread between the rich and the poor that Europe had at that time or that we have at present; a much larger proportion of society owned property then than now. Yet today, many people, even including many laborers, look on American society as predominately middle class, though the opportunity for almost universal ownership of property is far less now than it was before the Revolution.

Economic opportunity, or economic democracy, in turn contributed to political democracy. While it is true that property ownership was a prerequisite for province and town voting, it is also true that the amount of property required for the franchise was very small and that the great majority of men could easily meet the requirements. There were probably a few men who could not qualify for voting, but the number could not have been very large. We cannot condone the practice of excluding even those few, but we should try to place the unenfranchised in their proper perspective. It makes a tremendous difference in our understanding of colonial society whether 95 percent of the men were disfranchised or only 5 percent. Furthermore, representation was apportioned in such a way that the farmers, not a merchant aristocracy, had complete control of the legislature.

It is not enough to say that the people of Massachusetts perhaps had more democracy than the people of Europe, but that they still did not have what we call democracy today. Neither is it sufficient to say that the germs of democracy were present, or that democracy, as a growing process if not as a reality, could be found in colonial times. When Hutchinson said that anything that looked like a man was a voter and that policy in general was dictated by the lower classes, he was certainly using the term "democracy" as we mean it now. A Hutchinson might deplore the view that government existed for the benefit of the people and that the people were to decide when government had served its proper functions, but this is the democratic idea. He might also deplore the fact that the people not only elected their representatives but also told them how to vote, yet this, too, is democracy.

In many respects, the people of Massachusetts had a government more responsive to the popular will than we have at the present time. There were far more representatives in proportion to population than we now have, and the representatives were more responsible to their constituents for their actions than are legislators at present. If a man votes against his belief to please his constituents so that he can hold his elected position, we cannot demand much more of democracy.

The number of men who could vote in the colony must not be confused with the number who did vote. These are entirely different problems, for the fact that there was much indifference on election day did not mean that many men could not participate. If we are attempting to explain events in terms of class conflict or internal revolution, it is especially important that we do not confuse the unfranchised and the disinterested. It is one thing if a man wants the vote but cannot meet the property requirements; it is another if he has the vote but fails to use it. Neither should we confuse the issue by giving percentages of voters in terms of the entire population, for probably less than 20 percent of the people in colonial times were adult men.

In addition to economics and politics, there were also other manifestations of democracy in colonial Massachusetts. The system of education was, for its day, undoubtedly the best provided for the common people anywhere, and the correct comparison is with other educational systems at the time, not with our own. Many democratic practices were used in the operation of the Congregational church, and again we should remember that some 98 percent of the people were Congregationalists. Furthermore, the Congregational church was not established as it was in England.[1] Men who belonged to other churches did not pay taxes to the Congregational church; education and political office were open to those who were not Congregationalists. Perhaps there was not the complete religious freedom—or religious indifference—that we now associate with a liberal society, but there was also little dissatisfaction with religion to contribute to internal conflict. Even the colonial militia was democratic in its organization and in the influence which it exerted on politics.

In brief, Massachusetts did not have a social order before the American Revolution which would breed sharp internal class conflicts. The evidence does not justify an interpretation of the Revolution in Massachusetts as an internal class conflict designed to achieve additional political, economic, and social democracy. Although democracy was important as a factor in the conflict, it was a democracy which had already arrived in the colony long before 1776. . . .

Obviously democracy played an important part in the events before 1776, not as a condition to be achieved but as a reality which interfered with British policies. If the British had been successful, there would undoubtedly have been much less democracy in Massachusetts—hence the interpretation that the Revolution was designed to *preserve* a social order rather than to change it. We search in vain for evidence of class conflict that was serious enough to justify revolution; we do not have to look far for copious quantities of proof that colonial society was democratic and that the colonists were attempting to prevent British innovations.

[1] Brown here presumably refers to the establishment in England of the Anglican Church.

Furthermore, the results of the Revolution more than confirm the interpretation presented here. There is a logic to what happened after the Revolution—or perhaps it would be more accurate to say what did not happen—if we accept the fact that the people of Massachusetts were not conducting an internal revolution. We are not confronted with the contradiction, which most writers fail to resolve, of a social revolution which was presumably successful but which failed to achieve social change. Why would a people, who were supposedly demanding a more democratic government, adopt a constitution which restricted democracy even more than it had been restricted in colonial days? On the other hand, the Massachusetts Constitution of 1780 was a logical consequence of a middle-class society which believed in the protection of property because most men were property owners. The almost complete absence of social revolution in Massachusetts should stand as convincing evidence that internal social revolution was not one of the chief aims of the American Revolution as far as the people of Massachusetts were concerned.

It is not necessary to explain whatever conservatism existed in colonial times in terms of a limited electorate. There is implied in this approach an assumption that universal suffrage will result in increased liberalism, but this is not necessarily so. The elections of 1920, 1924, 1928, and even 1952, when women as well as men had the vote, should convince us that "the people" can and do vote for conservatism. If the people of Massachusetts believed that a man should own property to be a voter or that an official should be a Protestant to be elected to office, they might well vote for both propositions and not be out of character. And since most men in Massachusetts were Protestants and property owners, the fact that both property and religious qualifications found their way into the Constitution of 1780 should not be surprising.

We do not need a "conservative counterrevolution" or a thermidorean reaction to explain either the Massachusetts Constitution of 1780 or the adoption of the federal Constitution in 1788. If there was no "social revolution," there could hardly be a "conservative counterrevolution." Both constitutions must be explained in terms of a middle-class society in which most men could vote.

10

Merrill Jensen

"The American Revolution was a democratic movement, not in origin, but in result"

Merrill Jensen, who has done most of his writing while at the University of Wisconsin, claimed in his Articles of Confederation (1940) *and* The New Nation (1950) *that the American Revolution was characterized by a movement toward greater political democracy. When, during the 1950's, some of the neo-Whig historians questioned whether there had been important democratic gains from the revolutionary movement, Jensen wrote the article that follows, in which he reiterated his earlier position with some modifications.*

The historian who ventures to talk about democracy in early America is in danger because there are almost as many opinions as there are writers on the subject. The Puritans have been pictured as the founders of American democracy, and it is vigorously denied that they had anything to do with it. Some have seen in Roger Williams the father of American democracy, and others have denied that he was a democrat, whatever his putative progeny may be. The conflict is equally obvious when it comes to the American Revolution, and the problems of

SOURCE. Merrill Jensen "Democracy and the American Revolution," *The Huntington Library Quarterly*, **20** (1957), 321–341. Reprinted by permission of the author and publisher.

solution are far more complex than they are for the seventeenth century. The difficulty is compounded, for all too often men's emotions seem to become involved.

It is sometimes suggested that we avoid the use of the word "democracy" when discussing the seventeenth and eighteenth centuries. It seems to me that this is a flat evasion of the problem, for the Americans of those centuries used the word and they meant something by it. Our task, then, is not to avoid the issue but to try to understand what they meant, and understand what they meant in the context of the times in which they lived. What we must not do is to measure the seventeenth and eighteenth centuries in terms of our own assumptions about what democracy is or should be. This is all the more important since many of us do not seem to be too clear about our assumptions, even for the century in which we live.

A number of years ago I took the position that "in spite of the paradoxes involved one may still maintain that the Revolution was essentially, though relatively, a democratic movement within the thirteen American colonies, and that its significance for the political and constitutional history of the United States lay in its tendency to elevate the political and economic status of the majority of the people." And then, with a somewhat rhetorical flourish which I have sometimes regretted but have not as yet withdrawn, I went on to say that "the Articles of Confederation were the constitutional expression of this movement and the embodiment in governmental form of the philosophy of the Declaration of Independence." One thing can be said for this statement at least: reviewers read it and quoted it, some with raised eyebrows, and some with approval, whether or not they said anything at all about the rest of the book.

During most of the present century historians have assumed that democracy was involved somehow or other in the American Revolution. They have assumed also that there were conditions within the American colonies that were not satisfactory to at least some of the American people. The causes of internal discontent were various, ranging all the way from religious to economic differences. The discontent was of such intensity that in certain colonies it led to explosive outbreaks in the

1760's such as the Regulator movements in the Carolinas, the Paxton Boys' uprising in Pennsylvania, and the tenant farmer revolt in New York, outbreaks that were suppressed by the armed forces of the colonial governments and with the help of British power.

Most historians have agreed also that the individual colonies were controlled politically by relatively small groups of men in each of them, allied by family, or economic or political interests, or by some combination of these. The colonial aristocracies owed their position to many things: to their wealth and ability, to their family connections and political allies, and to the British government which appointed them to office. As opposed to Britain, they had won virtual self-government for the colonies by 1763. Yet in every colony they were a minority who managed to maintain internal control through property qualifications for the suffrage, especially effective in the growing towns, and through refusal or failure to grant representation in any way proportional to the population of the rapidly growing frontier areas. Probably more important than either of these was the fact that in most colonies the aristocracies manned the upper houses of the legislatures, the supreme courts, and other important posts—all by royal appointment. Beyond this, their control extended down through the county court system, even in Massachusetts. In short, colonial political society was not democratic in operation despite the elective lower houses and the self-government which had been won from Great Britain.

This is a brief but, I think, fair summary of a widely held point of view concerning the political actualities at the beginning of the revolutionary era.

This view has been challenged recently. A writer on Massachusetts declared that "as far as Massachusetts is concerned, colonial society and the American Revolution must be interpreted in terms something very close to a complete democracy with the exception of British restraints." It was not controlled by a wealthy aristocracy. There was little inequality of representation, and property was so widely held that virtually every adult male could vote.[1] The assumption that Massachusetts was an idyllic democracy, united in the fight against British tyranny, will be somewhat surprising to those who have read the letters of Francis Bernard and the diary of John Adams, not to mention the history of Thomas Hutchinson, and, I suspect, would be even more surprising to those gentlemen as well. Elsewhere, this writer has implied that what was true for Massachusetts was probably true for other colonies and for the United States after the Revolution.

On the other hand it is asserted that democracy had nothing to do with the Revolution. Such an assertion made in connection with Pennsylvania is a little startling, for ever since C. H. Lincoln's work of more than a half century ago, down to the present, it has been held that there was a democratic movement in Pennsylvania during the revolutionary era. Not so, says a reviewer of the most recent study. He declares that "the attribution of democratic motivations and ideas to eighteenth century colonists is a common fault among many historians of the colonial period. . . ." He argues that the struggle in Pennsylvania before 1776 was one between "radical and conservative variants of whiggism," which he defines as one between "those who held privilege most dear and those who valued property above all." The Pennsylvania Constitution of 1776 itself was not democratic, but a triumph of "colonial radical whiggism."

It is clear that a considerable diversity of opinion prevails. It is also clear that the time has come to set forth certain propositions or generalizations which seem to me to have a measure of validity.

First of all, a definition of democracy is called for. And just to face the issue squarely, I will offer one stated at Newport, Rhode Island, in 1641 when a meeting declared that "the government which this body politic doth attend unto . . . is a democracy or popular government; . . . that is to say: It is in the power of the body of freemen, orderly assembled, or the major

---

[1] Robert E. Brown, "Democracy in Colonial Massachusetts," *New England Quarterly*, XXV (1952), 291–303, and at length in *Middle-Class Democracy and the Revolution in Massachusetts, 1691–1780* (Ithaca, N. Y., 1955).

part of them, to make or constitute just laws, by which they will be regulated, and to depute from among themselves such ministers as shall see them faithfully executed between man and man.". . . .

The second proposition is that colonial governments on the eve of the Revolution did not function democratically, nor did the men who controlled them believe in democracy. Even if we agree that there was virtually manhood suffrage in Massachusetts, it is difficult, for me at least, to see it as a democracy. In 1760 the government was controlled by a superb political machine headed by Thomas Hutchinson, who with his relatives and political allies occupied nearly every important political office in the colony except the governorship. The Hutchinson oligarchy controlled the superior court, the council, the county courts, and the justices of the peace; with this structure of appointive office spread throughout the colony, it was able to control the house of representatives elected by the towns. For six years after 1760 the popular party in Boston, lead by Oxenbridge Thacher and James Otis, suffered one defeat after another at the hands of the Hutchinson machine. The popular leaders in the town of Boston tried everything from slander to mob violence to get control of the government of the colony but it was not until after the Stamp Act crisis that they were able to win a majority of the house of representatives to their side. Even then, men like James Otis did not at first realize that the Stamp Act could be turned to advantage in the fight against the Hutchinson oligarchy. In terms of political support between 1760 and 1765, if Massachusetts had a democratic leader, that man was Thomas Hutchinson, a charge to which he would have been the first to issue a horrified denial.

The third proposition is that before 1774 or 1775 the revolutionary movement was not a democratic movement, except by inadvertence. The pamphleteers who wrote on political and constitutional questions, and the town and county meetings and legislatures that resolved endlessly between 1763 and 1774, were concerned with the formulation of constitutional arguments to defend the colonies and their legislatures from interference by parliament.

The colonial theorists wrote much about the British constitution, the rights of Englishmen, and even of the laws of nature, but they accepted the British assumption that colonial governments derived from British charters and commissions. Their essential concern was with the relationship that existed, or ought to exist, between the British government and the colonial governments, and not with the relationship between man as man, and government itself. Such writers showed no interest in domestic problems, and when it was suggested that the arguments against taxation by parliament were equally applicable to the taxation of under-represented areas in the colonies, or to dissenting religious groups, such suggestions were looked upon as being quite out of order.

The same indifference was displayed in the realm of political realities. The ardent leaders of the fight against British policies showed no interest in, or sympathy for, the discontent of back-country farmers or religious groups such as the Baptists. Instead, they temporarily joined with their political enemies to suppress or ignore it. Such sympathy as the discontented got, they got from the British government, or from colonial leaders charged with being tools of the British power.

The fact is that the popular leaders of the revolutionary movement had no program of domestic reform. Instead, their program was a combination of a continuous assault on the local office-holding aristocracies and an ardent attack on British policies; and in the course of time they identified one with the other. It is sometimes difficult to tell with which side of the program the popular leaders were more concerned. In Massachusetts, for instance, before 1765 they were so violent in their attack on Hutchinson that they prevented Massachusetts from joining the other colonies in making formal protests against British legislation.

The fourth proposition is related to the third. It is that although the popular leaders in the colonies showed no interest in internal political and social change, they were still able to build up a political following, particularly in the seacoast towns. They were superb organizers, propagandists with a touch of genius, and possessed of an almost demonic energy in their dual fight against the local political aristocracies and British policies. After a few false starts such as that of James Otis, who at first called the Virginia Stamp Act Resolves treason, the popular leaders took an extreme stand on the subject of colonial rights. The political aristocracies might object to British policies, as most of them did, but considering what they owed to British backing, they displayed an understandable caution, a caution that made it impossible for them to pose as patriotic leaders.

The popular leaders were also willing to take extreme measures in practical opposition to British policies, ranging all the way from mob violence to non-importation agreements forced upon unwilling merchants. And with even more force and violence they accused Americans who did not agree with them or their methods of knuckling under to British tyranny and of readiness to sell the liberties of their country for a little pelf. In the course of this campaign they appealed to the people at large. Men who normally could not or did not take part in political life, particularly in the cities, were invited to mass meetings where the rules of suffrage were ignored and where they could shout approval of resolutions carefully prepared in advance by their leaders. In addition, the mob was a constant factor in political life, particularly in Boston where it was efficiently organized. Mobs were used to nullify the Stamp Act, to harass British soldiers, to hamper the operations of the customs service, and to intimidate office holders.

All these activities on the part of the disfranchised, or the hitherto politically inactive, accustomed men to taking part in political affairs as never before; and it gave them an appetite for more. From the beginning of the crisis in 1774 onward, more and more "new men," which was the politest name their opponents called them, played an ever more active role, both on the level of practical politics and on the level of political theory. They began writing about and talking about what they called "democracy." And this was a frightening experience, not only to the conservative-minded leaders of the colonies, but to many of the popular leaders as well.

For instance, when a New York mass meeting gathered in May 1774 to answer the letter of the Boston Town Meeting asking for a complete stoppage of trade with Britain as an answer to the Boston Port Act, the people talked about far more than letter writing. One alarmed observer wrote: "I beheld my fellow-citizens very accurately counting all their chickens, not only before any of them were hatched, but before above one half of the eggs were laid. In short, they fairly contended about the future forms of our government, whether it should be founded upon aristocratic or democratic principles." The leaders had "gulled" the mob for years, and now, said Gouverneur Morris, the mob was waking up and could no longer be fooled. The only salvation for the aristocracy of New York was peace with Britain at almost any price.

Another witness to the stirrings among the people was John Adams. Unlike Gouverneur Morris, he never wavered in his belief in independence, but at the same time he was constantly concerned with the danger of an internal upheaval. . . .

In May of 1776, with the talk of independence filling the air and the Virginia convention planning to draft a constitution, old Landon Carter of Virginia wrote to Washington bewailing the "ambition" that had "seized on so much ignorance all over the colony as it seems to have done; for this present convention abounds with too many of the inexperienced creatures to navigate our bark on this dangerous coast. . . ." As for independence, he said, "I need only tell you of one definition that I heard of Independency: It was expected to be a form of government that, by being independent of the rich men, every man would then be able to do as he pleased. And it was with this expectation they sent the men they did, in hopes they would plan such a form. One of the delegates I heard exclaim against the Patrolling Law, because a poor man was made to pay for keeping a rich man's slaves in order. I shamed the fool so much for it that he slunk away, but he got elected by it."

One could go on endlessly giving examples like these from the hectic days between 1774 and 1776, examples of the fear among leaders of all shades of opinion that the people would get or were getting out of hand. . . .

By early 1776 the debate over future governments to be adopted was in full swing. Disliking intensely the ideas of government set forth in *Common Sense,* John Adams drafted his *Thoughts on Government.* His plan was modeled on the old government of Massachusetts, with an elective rather than a royal governor, of course, but it certainly contemplated no radical change in the political structure. John Adams was no innovator. He deplored what he called "the rage for innovation" which had appeared in Massachusetts by June of 1776. The projects, said he, are not for repairing the building but for tearing it down. "The projects of county assemblies, town registers, and town probates of wills are founded in narrow notions, sordid stinginess, and profound ignorance, and tend directly to barbarism."

There was equal alarm in the south at demands for change and new governments. Among those who sought to defend the old order was Carter Braxton. In a long address to the Virginia convention he praised the British constitution and declared that it would be "perverting all order to oblige us; by a novel government, to give up our laws, our customs, and our manners." The spirit or principles of limited monarchy should be preserved. Yet, he said, we daily see it condemned by the advocates of "popular governments. . . . The systems recommended to the colonies seem to accord with the temper of the times, and are fraught with all the tumult and riot incident to simple democracy. . . ." Braxton declared that democracies would not tolerate wealth, and that they could exist only in countries where all the people are poor from necessity. Nowhere in history could he find an example of a successful democracy. What he proposed for Virginia was a three-part government with a house of representatives elected by the voters for three years. The house, in turn, would choose a governor to serve during good behavior and a council of twenty-four to hold their places for life and to act as an upper house of the legislature. Braxton in Virginia, like John Adams in Massachusetts, hoped to make the transition from dependence to independence without any fundamental political change.

But change was in the air, and writer after writer sought to formulate new ideas about government and to offer concrete suggestions for the theoretical foundations and political structures of the new states to be. In 1775, on hearing that congress had given advice to New Hampshire on the establishment of a government, General John Sullivan offered his thoughts to the revolutionary congress of his colony. All government, he wrote, ought to be instituted for the good of the people. There should be no conflicting branches in imitation of the British constitution "so much celebrated by those who understand nothing of it. . . ." The two houses of the legislature and a governor should all be elected by the people. No danger can arise to a state "from giving the people a free and full voice in their own government." The so-called checks upon the licentiousness of the people "are only the children of designing or ambitious men, no such thing being necessary. . . ."

In the middle colonies appeared an address "To the People of North America on the Different Kinds of Government." After defining monarchy, aristocracy, oligarchy, and democracy, the anonymous writer said: "Popular government—sometimes termed democracy, republic, or commonwealth—is the plan of civil society wherein the community at large takes the care of its own welfare, and manages its concerns by representatives elected by the people out of their own body."

"Seeing the happiness of the people is the true end of government; and it appearing by the definition, that the popular form is the only one which has this for its object; it may be worth inquiring into the causes which have prevented its success in the world."

This writer then undertakes to explain the failure of former democracies. First of all, he says that past republics tried democracy too late and contained within them remnants of aristocracies and military cliques which disliked it. A second cause was that men did not have adequate knowledge of representation and that their large and tumultuous assemblies made it possible for unscrupulous men to charge all troubles to the constitution. A third cause of failure has been the political writers who from ignorance or ulterior motives have tried to discredit democracy. "This has been carried to such a length with many, that the mentioning a democracy constantly excites in them the idea of anarchy; and few, except such as have emancipated themselves from the shackles of political bigotry and prejudice, can talk of it with patience, and hearken to anything offered in its defence." Such are the causes of the destruction of former republics, but the Americans have the best opportunity ever open to mankind to form a free government, "the last and best plan that can possibly exist.". . . .

In New England, where the revolutionary congresses of Massachusetts and New Hampshire were controlled by leaders along the seacoast, there was a growing discontent among the people of the back-country counties. Out of it came one of the clearest democratic statements of the times: "The People are the Best Governors." The author starts with the premise that "there are many very noisy about liberty, but are aiming at nothing more than personal power and grandeur." "God," he said, "gave mankind freedom by nature, made every man equal to his neighbor, and has virtually enjoined them to govern themselves by their own laws." Representatives in legislatures should have only the power to make laws. They should not have power to elect officials or to elect councils or senates to veto legislation. Only the people have this power. If there must be senates, they should be elected by the people of the state at large and should have only advisory powers. Representation should not be according to taxable property, for "Nature itself abhors such a system of civil government, for it will make an inequality among the people and set up a number of lords over the rest.". . . .

From such discussions one may sum up certain of the essential ideas. (1) They agree that the "good" or the "happiness" of the people is the only end of government. (2) They agree that "democracy" is the best form of government to achieve that end. (3) They show a distrust of men when in power—a distrust shared with far more conservative-minded writers of the times.

As to details of government there are variations, but they do agree on fundamentals. (1) The legislatures, whether one or two houses, are to be elected by the people. (2) Public officials, state and local, are to be elected by the people or by their representatives in the legislatures. (3) There should be annual elections. (4) Some argue for manhood suffrage, and one writer even advocated that tax-paying widows should vote. (5) There should be freedom of religion, at least for Protestants; in any case, freedom from taxation to support established churches.

One may well ask: did such theoretical discussions have any meaning in terms of practical politics, or were they idle speculations by anonymous writers without influence? The answer is that they did have meaning.... By the end of 1775 all sorts of organized activity was under way, ranging in place from North Carolina to New Hampshire, and from militia groups to churches.

In North Carolina the defeat of the Regulators in 1771 had not ended discontent but merely suppressed it. By September 1775 Mecklenburg County was instructing its delegates in the provincial congress to work for a plan of government providing for equal representation and the right to vote for every freeman who supported the government, either in person or property. Legislation should not be a "divided right"; no man or body of men should be "invested with a negative on the voice of the people duly collected...." By November 1776, when North Carolina elected a congress to write its first state constitution, Mecklenburg County was even more specific in its instructions. It told its delegates that they were to endeavor to establish a free government under the authority of the people of North Carolina, and that the government was to be a "simple democracy, or as near it as possible." In fixing fundamental principles, the delegates were to "oppose everything that leans to aristocracy or power in the hands of the rich and chief men exercised to the oppression of the poor."

In the middle colonies militia organizations made demands and suggestions. Pennsylvania was in turmoil, with the assembly controlled by the opponents of independence and the revolutionary party working in large measure through a voluntary militia organization called the Associators. In February 1776 a committee of privates from the Philadelphia Associators told the assembly "that it has been the practice of all countries, and is highly reasonable, that all persons ... who expose their lives in the defense of a country, should be admitted to the enjoyment

of all the rights and privileges of a citizen of that country. . . ."
All Associators should be given the right to vote. . . .

While such ideas were being expounded in Pennsylvania,
some militia in Maryland were proposing a new constitution.
There was a growing discontent in Maryland with the revolutionary convention which was opposed to independence, and
whose members were appointing one another to military posts.
Government by convention should stop, said one writer, and
regular government be instituted.

Late in June 1776 deputies from the militia battalions in
Anne Arundel County met and proposed a constitution to be
submitted to the people of the county. They started out with
the declaration that the right to legislate is in "every member
of the community," but that for convenience the right must be
delegated to representatives chosen by the people. The legislature must never form a separate interest from the community
at large, and its branches must "be independent of and balance
each other, and all dependent on the people." There should be
a two-house legislature chosen annually "as annual elections
are most friendly to liberty, and the oftener power reverts to the
people, the greater will be the security for a faithful discharge
of it." All provincial officials, including judges, should be
elected annually by joint ballot of the two houses. All county
officials should be chosen annually by the people of each county.
Nothing is said of property qualifications for either voting or
office-holding. So far as taxes are concerned, "the unjust mode
of taxation by poll" should be abolished, and all monies raised
should be according to a fair and equal assessment of people's
estates.

In New Jersey the revolutionary congress, like that in other
colonies, was trying to prevent change and was maintaining
the land qualification for voting for its members. But the
complaints grew so loud that it was forced to yield. One peti-
tion in 1776, for instance, declared that "we cannot conceive
the wise author of our existence ever designed that a certain
quantity of earth on which we tread should be annexed to a
man to complete his dignity and fit him for society. Was the
sole design of government either the security of land or money,

the possession of either or both of these would be the only necessary qualifications for its members. But we apprehend the benign intentions of a well regulated government to extend to the security of much more valuable possessions—the rights and privileges of freemen, for the defense of which every kind of property and even life itself have been liberally expended.". . . .

The Declaration of Independence was taken seriously by many Americans, or at least they found its basic philosophy useful in battling for change in the new states. Nowhere was this done more neatly than in Grafton County, New Hampshire. The Provincial Congress was in the control of eastern leaders and they refused to grant representation that the western towns thought adequate. In calling elections in the fall of 1776, the Congress grouped various towns together for electing representatives and told them that the men they elected must own real estate worth £200 lawful money. Led by professors at an obscure little college at Hanover, the people of Grafton County went on strike. They refused to hold elections, and town after town met and passed resolutions. The whole procedure of the Congress was unconstitutional. No plan of representation had been adopted since the Declaration of Independence. By the Declaration, said Hanover and two other towns in a joint statement, "we conceive that the powers of government reverted to the people at large, and of course annihilated the political existence of the Assembly which then was. . . ." Six other towns joined together and declared it to be "our humble opinion, that when the declaration of independency took place, the Colonies were absolutely in a state of nature, and the powers of government reverted to the people at large. . . ." Such being the case, the Provincial Congress has no authority to combine towns, each of which is entitled to representation as a corporate entity. And it has no right to limit the choice of representatives to the owners of £200, said the people of Lyme, because "every elector in free states is capable of being elected."

It seems clear, to me at least, that by 1776 there were people in America demanding the establishment of democratic state governments, by which they meant legislatures controlled by a majority of the voters, and with none of the checks upon their actions such as had existed in the colonies. At the same time there were many Americans who were determined that there should be no changes except those made inevitable by separation from Great Britain.

The history of the writing of the first state constitutions is to a large extent the history of the conflict between these two ideals of government. The conflict can be exaggerated, of course, for there was considerable agreement on structural details. Most of the state constitutions worked out in written form the structure of government that had existed in the colonies, all the way from governors, two-house legislatures, and judicial systems, to the forms of local government. In terms of structure, little that is revolutionary is to be found. Even the much maligned unicameral legislature of Pennsylvania was only a continuation of what Pennsylvania had had since the beginning of the century.

The significant thing is not the continuity of governmental structure, but the alteration of the balance of power within the structure, and in the political situation resulting from the break away from the supervising power of a central government —that of Great Britain.

The first and most revolutionary change was in the field of basic theory. In May 1776, to help bring about the overthrow of the Pennsylvania assembly, the chief stumbling block in the way of independence, Congress resolved that all governments exercising authority under the crown of Great Britain should be suppressed, and that "all the powers of government [be] exerted under the authority of the people of the colonies. . . ." John Adams described it as "the most important resolution that ever was taken in America." The Declaration of Independence spelled it out in terms of the equality of men, the sovereignty of the people, and the right of a people to change their governments as they pleased.

Second: the Revolution ended the power of a sovereign central government over the colonies. Britain had had the power to appoint and remove governors, members of upper houses of legislatures, judges, and other officials. It had the power to veto colonial legislation, to review cases appealed from colonial supreme courts, and to use armed force. All of this superintending power was wiped out by independence.

Third: the new central government created in America by the Articles of Confederation was, in a negative sense at least, a democratic government. The Congress of the United States had no power over either the states or their citizens. Hence, each state could govern itself as it pleased, and as a result of some of the new state constitutions, this often meant by a majority of the voters within a state.

Fourth: in writing the state constitutions, change was inevitable. The hierarchy of appointed legislative, executive, and judicial officials which had served as a check upon the elective legislatures was gone. The elective legislature became the supreme power in every state, and the lower houses, representing people however inadequately, became the dominant branch. The appointive houses of colonial times were replaced by elective senates, which in theory were supposed to represent property. They were expected to, and sometimes did, act as a check upon the lower houses, but their power was far less than that of pre-war councils.

Fifth: the office of governor underwent a real revolution. The governors of the royal colonies had, in theory at least, vast powers including an absolute veto. In the new constitutions, most Americans united in shearing the office of governor of virtually all power.

Sixth: state supreme courts underwent a similar revolution. Under the state constitutions they were elected by the legislatures or appointed by governors who were elected officials. And woe betide a supreme court that tried to interfere with the actions of a legislature.

What such changes meant in terms of political realities was that a majority of voters within a state, if agreed upon a program and persistent enough, could do what it wanted, unchecked by governors or courts or appeals to a higher power outside the state.

There were other areas in which changes took place, although they were only beginnings. A start was made in the direction of ending the property qualification for voting and office-holding.   A few states established what amounted to manhood suffrage, and a few years later even women voted in New Jersey although that was stopped when it appeared that woman suffrage meant only a means of stuffing ballot boxes. A few states took steps in the direction of representation according to population, a process as yet unsolved in the United States. A large step was taken in the direction of disestablishing state churches, but on the whole one still had to be a Protestant, and a Trinitarian at that, to hold office.

In connection with office-holding, there is one eighteenth-century American idea that is worthy of a whole study by itself, and that is the concept of rotation in office. Many Americans were convinced that office-holding bred a lust for power in the holder. Therefore there must be frequent, if not annual, elections; and there must be a limitation on the time one might spend in certain offices. There is probably no more remarkable self-denying ordinance in the history of politics than the provision in the Articles of Confederation that no man could be a member of Congress more than three years out of any six. I have often been accused of wanting to go back to the Articles of Confederation, which is nonsense, but there are times when I do wish that this one provision might be revived in the twentieth century.

What I have done in this paper is to set before you some of the reasons for believing that the American Revolution was a democratic movement, not in origin, but in result. Certainly the political leaders of the eighteenth century thought the results were democratic. Whether they thought the results were good or bad is another story.

11 Bernard Bailyn
"The ultimate explanation of every political controversy was the disposition of power"

The renewed interest that has developed during the last twenty-five years in the intellectual origins of the American Revolution is well shown in the work of Bernard Bailyn. Professor of History at Harvard University, Bailyn undertook an intensive study of the ideas that appeared in the revolutionary movement while working on his projected four-volume Pamphlets of the American Revolution, *of which the first volume was published in 1965. He attempted to separate and to understand the various threads of American political thought that became the basis of radical action. From widely scattered sources he tried to distill something of the psychological hopes and fears that lay the groundwork for violent revolution.*

The theory of politics that emerges from the political literature of the pre-Revolutionary years rests on the belief that what lay behind every political scene, the ultimate explanation of every

SOURCE. Reprinted by permission of the publishers from Bernard Bailyn, *The Ideological Origins of the American Revolution,* pp. 55–67. Cambridge, Mass.: The Belknap Press of Harvard University Press. Copyright © 1967 by the President and Fellows of Harvard College.

political controversy, was the disposition of power. The acuteness of the colonists' sense of this problem is, for the twentieth-century reader, one of the most striking things to be found in this eighteenth-century literature: it serves to link the Revolutionary generation to our own in the most intimate way.

The colonists had no doubt about what power was and about its central, dynamic role in any political system. Power was not to be confused, James Otis pointed out, with unspecified physical capacity—with the "mere physical quality" described in physics. The essence of what they meant by power was perhaps best revealed inadvertently by John Adams as he groped for words in drafting his *Dissertation on the Canon and Feudal Law*. Twice choosing and then rejecting the word "power," he finally selected as the specification of the thought he had in mind "dominion," and in this association of words the whole generation concurred. "Power" to them meant the dominion of some men over others, the human control of human life: ultimately force, compulsion. And it was, consequently, for them as it is for us "a richly connotative word": some of its fascination may well have lain for them, as it has been said to lie for us, in its "sado-masochistic flavor," for they dwelt on it endlessly, almost compulsively; it is referred to, discussed, dilated on at length and in similar terms by writers of all backgrounds and of all positions in the Anglo-American controversy.

Most commonly the discussion of power centered on its essential characteristic of aggressiveness: its endlessly propulsive tendency to expand itself beyond legitimate boundaries. In expressing this central thought, which explained more of politics, past and present, to them than any other single consideration, the writers of the time outdid themselves in verbal ingenuity. All sorts of metaphors, similes, and analogies were used to express this view of power. The image most commonly used was that of the act of trespassing. Power, it was said over and over again, has "an encroaching nature"; ". . . if at first it meets with no control [it] creeps by degrees and quick subdues the whole." Sometimes the image is of the human hand, "the hand of power," reaching out to clutch and to seize: power is "grasping" and "tenacious" in its nature; "what it seizes it will retain." Sometimes power "is like the ocean, not easily admitting limits to be fixed in it." Sometimes it is "like a cancer, it eats faster and faster every hour." Sometimes it is motion, desire, and appetite all at once, being "restless, aspiring, and insatiable." Sometimes it is like "jaws . . . always open to devour." It is everywhere in public life, and everywhere it is threatening, pushing, and grasping; and too often in the end it destroys its benign—necessarily benign—victim.

What gave transcendent importance to the aggressiveness of power was the fact that its natural prey, its necessary victim, was liberty, or law, or right. The public world these writers saw was divided into distinct, contrasting, and innately antagonistic spheres: the sphere of power and the sphere of liberty or right. The one was brutal, ceaselessly active, and heedless; the other was delicate, passive, and sensitive. The one must be resisted, the other defended, and the two must never be confused. "Right and power," Richard Bland stated, "have very different meanings, and convey very different ideas"; "power abstracted from right cannot give a just title to dominion," nor is it possible legitimately, or even logically, to "build right upon power." When the two are intermingled, when "brutal power" becomes "an irresistible argument of boundless right" as it did, John Dickinson explained, under the Cromwellian dictatorship, innocence and justice can only sigh and quietly submit.

Not that power was in itself—in some metaphysical sense—evil. It was natural in its origins, and necessary. It had legitimate foundations "in compact and mutual consent"—in those covenants among men by which, as a result of restrictions voluntarily accepted by all for the good of all, society emerges from a state of nature and creates government to serve as trustee and custodian of the mass of surrendered individual powers. Power created legitimately by those voluntary compacts which the colonists knew from Lockean theory to be logical and from their own experience to be practical, power in its legitimate form inhered naturally in government and was the possession and interest of those who controlled government, just as liberty, always weak, always defensive, always, as John Adams put it, "skulking about in corners . . . hunted and persecuted in all countries by cruel power," inhered naturally in the people and was their peculiar possession and interest. Liberty was not, therefore, for the colonists, as it is for us, professedly the interest and concern of all, governors and governed alike, but only of the governed. The wielders of power did not speak for it, nor did they naturally serve it. Their interest was to use and develop power, no less natural and necessary than liberty but more dangerous. For "as great a blessing as government is," the Rev. Peter Whitney explained, "like other blessings, it may become a scourge, a curse, and severe punishment to a people." What made it so, what turned power into a malignant force, was not its own nature so much as the nature of man— his susceptibility to corruption and his lust for self-aggrandizement.

On this there was absolute agreement. Everyone, of course, knew that if "weak or ignorant men are entrusted with power" there will be "universal confusion," for "such exaltation will ... make them giddy and vain and deprive them of the little understanding they had before." But it was not simply a question of what the weak and ignorant will do. The problem was more systematic than that; it concerned "mankind in general." And the point they hammered home time and again, and agreed on—freethinking Anglican literati no less than neo-Calvinist theologians—was the incapacity of the species, of mankind in general, to withstand the temptations of power. Such is "the depravity of mankind," Samuel Adams, speaking for the Boston Town Meeting, declared, "that ambition and lust of power above the law are ... predominant passions in the breasts of most men." These are instincts that have "in all nations combined the worst passions of the human heart and the worst projects of the human mind in league against the liberties of mankind." Power always and everywhere had had a pernicious, corrupting effect upon men. It "converts a good man in private life to a tyrant in office." It acts upon men like drink: it "is known to be intoxicating in its nature"—"too intoxicating and liable to abuse." And nothing within man is sufficiently strong to guard against these effects of power— certainly not "the united considerations of reason and religion," for they have never "been sufficiently powerful to restrain these lusts of men."

From these central premises on the nature of power and man's weakness in face of its temptations, there followed a series of important conclusions. Since power "in proportion to its extent is ever prone to wantonness," Josiah Quincy wrote, and since in the last analysis "the supreme power is ever possessed by those who have arms in their hands and are disciplined to the use of them," the absolute danger to liberty lay in the absolute supremacy of "a veteran army"—making "the civil subordinate to the military," as Jefferson put it in 1774, "instead of subjecting the military to the civil powers." Their fear was not simply of armies but of *standing armies,* a phrase that had distinctive connotations, derived, like so much of their political thought, from the seventeenth century and articulated for them by earlier English writers—in this case most memorably by Trenchard in his famous *An Argument, Shewing, that a Standing Army Is Inconsistent with a Free Government . . .* (1697). With him the colonists universally agreed that "unhappy nations have lost that precious jewel *liberty* . . . [because] their necessities or indiscretion have permitted a standing army to be kept amongst them." There was, they knew, no "worse state of tharldom than a military power in any government, unchecked and uncontrolled by the civil power"; and they had a vivid sense of what such armies were: gangs of restless mercenaries, responsible only to the whims of the rulers who paid them, capable of destroying all right, law, and liberty that stood in their way.

This fear of standing armies followed directly from the colonists' understanding of power and of human nature: on purely logical grounds it was a reasonable fear. But it went beyond mere logic. Only too evidently was it justified, as the colonists saw it, by history and by the facts of the contemporary world. Conclusive examples of what happened when standing armies were permitted to dominate communities were constantly before their minds' eyes. There was, first and foremost, the example of the Turks, whose rulers—cruel, sensuous, "bashaws in their little divans"—were legendary, ideal types of despots who reigned unchecked by right or law or in any sense the consent of the people; their power rested on the swords of their vicious janissaries, the worst of standing armies. So too had the French kings snuffed out the liberties of their subjects "by force" and reduced to nothing the "puny privilege of the French parliaments." The ranks of "despotic kingdoms" included also Poland, Spain, and Russia; India and Egypt were occasionally mentioned too.

More interesting than these venerable despotisms, bywords for the rule of force unrestrained by countervailing influences, were a number of despotic states that had within living memory been free and whose enslavement, being recent, had been directly observed. Venice was one: it had once, not so long ago, been a republic, but now it was governed "by one of the worst of despotisms." Sweden was another; the colonists themselves could remember when the Swedish people had enjoyed liberty to the full; but now, in the 1760's, they were known to "rejoice at being subject to the caprice and arbitrary power of a tyrant, and kiss their chains." But the most vivid of these sad cases, because the most closely studied, was that of Denmark. The destruction of parliamentary liberties in Denmark had in fact taken place a century before, but that event, carefully examined in a treatise famous in opposition circles and in America, was experienced as contemporary by the colonists.

Molesworth's *An Account of Denmark* (1694) established the general point, implicit in all similar histories but explicit in this one, that the preservation of liberty rested on the ability of the people to maintain effective checks on the wielders of power, and hence in the last analysis rested on the vigilance and moral stamina of the people. Certain forms of government made particularly heavy demands on the virtue of the people. Everyone knew that democracy—direct rule by all the people— required such spartan, self-denying virtue on the part of all the people that it was likely to survive only where poverty made upright behavior necessary for the perpetuation of the race. Other forms, aristocracies, for example, made less extreme de- mands; but even in them virtue and sleepless vigilance on the part of at least the ruling class were necessary if privilege was to be kept responsible and the inroads of tyranny perpetually blocked off. It had been the lack of this vigilance that had brought liberty in Denmark to its knees, for there a corrupt nobility, more interested in using its privileges for self-indulgence than for service to the state, had dropped its guard and allowed in a standing army which quickly destroyed the constitution and the liberties protected by it.

The converse of all of this was equally true and more directly relevant. The few peoples that had managed to retain their liberties in the face of all efforts of would-be tyrants propelled by the lust for power had been doughty folk whose vigilance had never relaxed and whose virtue had remained uncontaminated. The Swiss, a rustic people locked in mountain sanctuaries, were ancient members of this heroic group; they had won their liberty long ago and had maintained it stubbornly ever after. The Dutch were more recent members, having overthrown the despotic rule of Spain only a century earlier; they too were industrious people of stubborn, Calvinist virtue, and they were led by an alert aristocracy. More recent in their emergence from darkness were the Corsicans, whose revolt against Genoese overlords backed by French power had begun only in 1729; they were still, at the time of the Stamp Act, struggling under the leadership of Pasquale Paoli to maintain their independence and liberty.

Above all, however, there were the English themselves. The colonists' attitude to the whole world of politics and government was fundamentally shaped by the root assumption that they, as Britishers, shared in a unique inheritance of liberty. The English people, they believed, though often threatened by despots who had risen in their midst, had managed to maintain, to a greater degree and for a longer period of time than any other people, a tradition of the successful control of power and of those evil tendencies of human nature that would prevent its proper uses.

In view of the natural obstacles that stood in the way of such a success and in view of the dismal history of other nations, this, as the colonists saw it, had been an extraordinary achievement. But it was not a miraculous one. It could be explained historically. The ordinary people of England, they believed, were descended from simple, sturdy Saxons who had known liberty in the very childhood of the race and who, through the centuries, had retained the desire to preserve it. But it had taken more than desire. Reinforcing, structuring, expressing the liberty-loving temper of the people, there was England's peculiar "constitution," described by John Adams, in words almost every American agreed with before 1763, as "the most perfect combination of human powers in society which finite wisdom has yet contrived and reduced to practice for the preservation of liberty and the production of happiness."

12 *Gordon S. Wood*

"We may be approaching a crucial juncture in our writing about the Revolution"

In the following article Gordon S. Wood of the University of Michigan attempts to find some accommodation between the comprehensive and detailed work that has been done by the "apparently discredited" socio-economic historians and the recent approaches to the American Revolution of the intellectual historians. In this essay Wood uses Bernard Bailyn's writings to represent the "culmination of the idealist approach to the history of the Revolution," and his analysis of Bailyn's methods offers an excellent background to his efforts to bridge the apparent gulf between two interpretations.

If any catch phrase is to characterize the work being done on the American Revolution by this generation of historians, it will probably be "the American Revolution considered as an intellectual movement." For we now seem to be fully involved in a phase of writing about the Revolution in which the thought of the Revolutionaries, rather than their social and economic interests, has become the major focus of research and analysis. This recent emphasis on ideas is not of course new, and indeed

SOURCE. Gordon S. Wood, "Rhetoric and Reality in the American Revolution," *William and Mary Quarterly*, 3d ser., 23 (January 1966), 3–16, 20–27, 31–32. Reprinted by permission of the author.

right from the beginning it has characterized almost all our
attempts to understand the Revolution. The ideas of a period
which Samuel Eliot Morison and Harold Laski once described
as, next to the English revolutionary decades of the seventeenth
century, the most fruitful era in the history of Western political
thought could never be completely ignored in any phase of
our history writing.

It has not been simply the inherent importance of the Revolutionary ideas, those "great principles of freedom," that has
continually attracted the attention of historians. It has been
rather the unusual nature of the Revolution and the constant
need to explain what on the face of it seems inexplicable that
has compelled almost all interpreters of the Revolution, including the participants themselves, to stress its predominantly
intellectual character and hence its uniqueness among Western
revolutions. Within the context of Revolutionary historiography
the one great effort to disparage the significance of ideas in
the Revolution—an effort which dominated our history writing
in the first half of the twentieth century—becomes something of
an anomaly, a temporary aberration into a deterministic social
and economic explanation from which we have been retreating
for the past two decades. Since roughly the end of World War
II we have witnessed a resumed and increasingly heightened
insistence on the primary significance of conscious beliefs, and
particularly of constitutional principles, in explaining what
once again has become the unique character of the American
Revolution. In the hands of idealistic-minded historians the
thought and principles of the Americans have consequently
come to repossess that explanative force which the previous
generation of materialists-minded historians had tried to locate
in the social structure.

Indeed, our renewed insistence on the importance of ideas
in explaining the Revolution has now attained a level of full-
ness and sophistication never before achieved, with the consequence that the economic and social approach of the previous
generation of behaviorist historians has never seemed more
anomalous and irrelevant than it does at present. Yet paradoxically it may be that this preoccupation with the explanatory

power of the Revolutionary ideas has become so intensive and
so refined, assumed such a character, that the apparently discredited social and economic approach of an earlier generation
has at the same time never seemed more attractive and relevant.
In other words, we may be approaching a crucial juncture in
our writing about the Revolution where idealism and behavior-
ism meet.

It was the Revolutionaries themselves who first described
the peculiar character of what they had been involved in. The
Revolution, as those who took stock at the end of three decades
of revolutionary activity noted, was not "one of those events
which strikes the public eye in the subversions of laws which
have usually attended the revolutions of governments." Because it did not seem to have been a typical revolution, the
sources of its force and its momentum appeared strangely un-
accountable. "In other revolutions, the sword has been drawn
by the arm of offended freedom, under an oppression that
threatened the vital powers of society." But this seemed hardly
true of the American Revolution. There was none of the
legendary tyranny that had so often driven desperate peoples
into revolution. The Americans were not an oppressed people;
they had no crushing imperial shackles to throw off. In fact, the
Americans knew they were probably freer and less burdened
with cumbersome feudal and monarchial restraints that any
part of mankind in the eighteenth century. To its victims, the
Tories, the Revolution was truly incomprehensible. Never in
history, said Daniel Leonard, had there been so much rebellion
with so "little real cause." It was, wrote Peter Oliver, "the most
wanton and unnatural rebellion that ever existed." The Americans' response was out of all proportion to the stimuli. The
objective social reality scarcely seemed capable of explaining
a revolution.

Yet no American doubted that there had been a revolution.
How then was it to be justified and explained? If the American
Revolution, lacking "those mad, tumultuous actions which dis-
graced many of the great revolutions of antiquity," was not a
typical revolution, what kind of revolution was it? If the origin

of the American Revolution lay not in the usual passions and interests of men, wherein did it lay? Those Americans who looked back at what they had been through could only marvel at the rationality and moderation, "supported by the energies of well weighed choice," involved in their separation from Britain, a revolution remarkably "without violence or convulsion." It seemed to be peculiarly an affair of the mind. Even two such dissimilar sorts of Whigs as Thomas Paine and John Adams both came to see the Revolution they had done so much to bring about as especially involved with ideas, resulting from "a mental examination," a change in "the minds and hearts of the people." The Americans were fortunate in being born at a time when the principles of government and freedom were better known than at any time in history. The Americans had learned "how to define the rights of nature,— how to search into, to distinguish, and to comprehend, the principles of physical, moral, religious, and civil liberty," how, in short, to discover and resist the forces of tyranny before they could be applied. Never before in history had a people achieved "a revolution by reasoning" alone.

The Americans, "born the heirs of freedom," revolted not to create but to maintain their freedom. American society had developed differently from that of the Old World. From the time of the first settlements in the seventeenth century, wrote Samuel Williams in 1794, "every thing tended to produce, and to establish the spirit of freedom." While the speculative philosophers of Europe were laboriously searching their minds in an effort to decide the first principles of liberty, the Americans had come to experience vividly that liberty in their everyday lives. The American Revolution, said Williams, joined together these enlightened ideas with America's experience. The Revolution was thus essentially intellectual and declaratory: it "explained the business to the world, and served to confirm what nature and society had before produced." "All was the result of reason. . . ." The Revolution had taken place not in a succession of eruptions that had crumbled the existing social structure, but in a succession of new thoughts and new ideas that had vindicated that social structure.

The same logic that drove the participants to view the Revolution as peculiarly intellectual also compelled Moses Coit Tyler, writing at the end of the nineteenth century, to describe the American Revolution as "preeminently a revolution caused by ideas, and pivoted on ideas." That ideas played a part in all revolutions Tyler readily admitted. But in most revolutions, like that of the French, ideas had been perceived and acted upon only when the social reality had caught up with them, only when the ideas had been given meaning and force by long-experienced "real evils." The American Revolution, said Tyler, had been different: it was directed "not against tyranny inflicted, but only against tyranny anticipated." The Americans revolted not out of actual suffering but out of reasoned principle. "Hence, more than with most other epochs of revolutionary strife, our epoch of revolutionary strife was a strife of ideas: a long warfare of political logic; a succession of annual campaigns in which the marshalling of arguments not only preceded the marshalling of armies, but often exceeded them in impression upon the final result."

It is in this historiographical context developed by the end of the nineteenth century, this constant and at times extravagant emphasis on the idealism of the Revolution, that the true radical quality of the Progressive generation's interpretation of the Revolution becomes so vividly apparent. For the work of these Progressive historians was grounded in a social and economic explanation of the Revolutionary era that explicitly rejected the causal importance of ideas. These historians could scarcely have avoided the general intellectual climate of the first part of the twentieth century which regarded ideas as suspect. By absorbing the diffused thinking of Marx and Freud and the assumptions of behaviorist psychology, men had come to conceive of ideas as ideologies or rationalizations, as masks obscuring the underlying interests and drives that actually determined social behavior. For too long, it seemed, philosophers had reified thought, detaching ideas from the material conditions that produced them and investing them with an independent will that was somehow alone responsible for the determination of events. As Charles Beard pointed out in his introduction to the 1935 edition of *An Economic Interpretation of the Constitution*, previous historians of the Constitution had assumed that ideas were "entities, particularities, or forces, apparently independent of all earthly considerations coming under the head of 'economic.'" It was Beard's aim, as it was the aim of many of his contemporaries, to bring into historical consideration "those realistic features of economic conflict, stress, and strain" which previous interpreters of the Revolution had largely ignored. The product of this aim was a generation or more of historical writing about the Revolutionary period (of which Beard's was but the most famous expression) that sought to explain the Revolution and the formation of the Constitution in terms of socio-economic relationships and interests rather than in terms of ideas.

Curiously, the consequence of this reversal of historical approaches was not the destruction of the old-fashioned conception of the nature of ideas. As Marx had said, he intended only to put Hegel's head in its rightful place; he had no desire to cut it off. Ideas as rationalization, as ideology, remained—still distinct entities set in opposition to interests, now however lacking any deep causal significance, becoming merely a covering superstructure for the underlying and determinative social reality. Ideas therefore could still be the subject of historical investigation, as long as one kept them in their proper place, interesting no doubt in their own right but not actually counting for much in the movement of events.

Even someone as interested in ideas as Carl Becker never seriously considered them to be in any way determinants of what happened. Ideas fascinated Becker, but it was as superstructure that he enjoyed examining them, their consistency, their logic, their clarity, the way men formed and played with them. In his *Declaration of Independence: A Study in the History of Political Ideas* the political theory of the Americans takes on an unreal and even fatuous quality. It was as if ideas were merely refined tools to be used by the colonists in the most adroit manner possible. The entire Declaration of Independence, said Becker, was calculated for effect, designed primarily "to convince a candid world that the colonies had a moral and legal right to separate from Great Britain." The severe indictment of the King did not spring from unfathomable passions but was contrived, conjured up, to justify a rebellion whose sources lay elsewhere. Men to Becker were never the victims of their thought, always the masters of it. Ideas were a kind of legal brief. "Thus step by step, from 1764 to 1776, the colonists modified their theory to suit their needs." The assumptions behind Becker's 1909 behaviorist work on New York politics in the Revolution and his 1922 study of the political ideas in the Declaration of Independence were more alike than they at first might appear.

Bringing to their studies of the Revolution similar assumptions about the nature of ideas, some of Becker's contemporaries went on to expose starkly the implications of those assumptions. When the entire body of Revolutionary thinking was examined, these historians could not avoid being struck by its generally bombastic and overwrought quality. The ideas expressed seemed so inflated, such obvious exaggerations of reality, that they could scarcely be taken seriously. The Tories were all "wretched hirelings, and execrable parricides"; George III, the "tyrant of the earth," a "monster in human form"; the British soldiers, "a mercenary, licentious rabble of banditti," intending to "tear the bowels and vitals of their brave but peaceable fellow subjects, and *to wash the ground with a profusion of innocent blood.*" Such extravagant language, it seemed, could be nothing but calculated deception, at best an obvious distortion of fact, designed to incite and mold a revolutionary fervor. "The stigmatizing of British policy as 'tyranny,' 'oppression' and 'slavery,'" wrote Arthur M. Schlesinger, the dean of the Progressive historians, "had little or no objective reality, at least prior to the Intolerable Acts, but ceaseless repetition of the charge kept emotions at fever pitch."

Indeed, so grandiose, so overdrawn, it seemed, were the ideas that the historians were necessarily led to ask not whether such ideas were valid but why men should have expressed them. It was not the content of such ideas but the function that was really interesting. The Revolutionary rhetoric, the profusion of sermons, pamphlets, and articles in the patriotic cause, could best be examined as propaganda, that is, as a concerted and self-conscious effort by agitators to manipulate and shape public opinion. Because of the Progressive historians' view of the Revolution as the movement of class minorities bent on promoting particular social and economic interests, the conception of propaganda was crucial to their explanation of what seemed to be a revolutionary consensus. Through the use of ideas in provoking hatred and influencing opinion and creating at least "an appearance of unity," the influence of a minority of agitators was out of all proportion to their number. The Revolution thus became a display of extraordinary skillfulness in the manipuation of public opinion. In fact, wrote Schlesinger, "no disaffected element in history has ever risen more splendidly to the occasion."

Ideas thus became, as it were, parcels of thought to be distributed and used where they would do the most good. This propaganda was not of course necessarily false, but it was always capable of manipulation. "Whether the suggestions are to be true or false, whether the activities are to be open or concealed," wrote Philip Davidson, "are matters for the propagandist to decide." Apparently ideas could be turned on or off at will, and men controlled their rhetoric in a way they could not control their interests. Whatever the importance of propaganda, its connection with social reality was tenuous. Since ideas were so self-consciously manageable, the Whigs were not actually expressing anything meaningful about themselves but were rather feigning and exaggerating for effect. What the Americans said could not be taken at face value but must be considered as a rhetorical disguise for some hidden interest. The expression of even the classic and well-defined natural rights philosophy became, in Davidson's view, but "the propagandist's rationalization of his desire to protect his vested interests."

With this conception of ideas as weapons shrewdly used by designing propagandists, it was inevitable that the thought of the Revolutionaries should have been denigrated. The Revolutionaries became by implication hypocritical demagogues, "adroitly tailoring their arguments to changing conditions." Their political thinking appeared to possess neither consistency nor significance. "At best," said Schlesinger in an early summary of his interpretation, "an exposition of the political theories of the anti-parliamentary party is an account of their retreat from one strategic position to another." So the Whigs moved, it was strongly suggested, easily if not frivolously from a defense of charter rights, to the rights of Englishmen, and finally to the rights of man, as each position was exposed and became untenable. In short, concluded Schlesinger, the Revolution could never be understood if it were regarded "as a great forensic controversy over abstract governmental rights."

It is essentially on this point of intellectual consistency that Edmund S. Morgan has fastened for the past decade and a half in an attempt to bring down the entire interpretive framework of the socio-economic argument. If it could be shown that the thinking of the Revolutionaries was not inconsistent after all, that the Whigs did not actually skip from one constitutional notion to the next, then the imputation of Whig frivolity and hypocrisy would lose its force. This was a central intention of Morgan's study of the political thought surrounding the Stamp Act. As Morgan himself has noted and others have repeated, "In the last analysis the significance of the Stamp Act crisis lies in the emergence, not of leaders and methods and organizations, but of well-defined constitutional principles." As early as 1765 the Whigs "laid down the line on which Americans stood until they cut their connections with England. Consistently from 1765 to 1776 they denied the authority of Parliament to tax them externally or internally; consistently they affirmed their willingness to submit to whatever legislation Parliament should enact for the supervision of the empire as a whole." This consistency thus becomes, as one scholar's survey of the current interpretation puts it, "an indication of American devotion to principle."

It seemed clear once again after Morgan's study that the Americans were more sincerely attached to constitutional principles than the behaviorist historians had supposed, and that their ideas could not be viewed as simply manipulated prop-

aganda. Consequently the cogency of the Progressive historians'
interpretation was weakened if not unhinged. And as the
evidence against viewing the Revolution as rooted in internal
class-conflict continued to mount from various directions, it
appeared more and more comprehensible to accept the old-
fashioned notion that the Revolution was after all the consequence of "a great forensic controversy over abstract governmental rights." There were, it seemed, no deprived and
depressed populace yearning for a participation in politics that
had long been denied; no coherent merchant class victimizing
a mass of insolvent debtors; no seething discontent with the
British mercantile system; no privileged aristocracy, protected
by law, anxiously and insecurely holding power against a
clamoring democracy. There was, in short, no internal class
upheaval in the Revolution.

If the Revolution was not to become virtually incomprehensible, it must have been the result of what the American Whigs
always contended it was—a dispute between Mother Country
and colonies over constitutional liberties. By concentrating on
the immediate events of the decade leading up to independence,
the historians of the 1950's have necessarily fled from the economic and social determinism of the Progressive historians. And
by emphasizing the consistency and devotion with which Americans held their constitutional beliefs they have once again
focused on what seems to be the extraordinary intellectuality
of the American Revolution and hence its uniqueness among
Western revolutions. This interpretation, which, as Jack P.
Greene notes, "may appropriately be styled neo-whig," has
turned the Revolution into a rationally conservative movement,
involving mainly a constitutional defense of existing political
liberties against the abrupt the unexpected provocations of the
British government after 1760. "The issue then, according to
the neo-whigs, was no more and no less than separation from
Britain and the preservation of American liberty." The Revolution has therefore become "more political, legalistic, and
constitutional than social or economic." Indeed, some of the
neo-Whig historians have implied not just that social and
economic conditions were less important in bringing on the

Revolution as we once thought, but rather that the social situation in the colonies had little or nothing to do with causing the Revolution. The Whig statements of principle iterated in numerous declarations appear to be the only causal residue after all the supposedly deeper social and economic causes have been washed away. As one scholar who has recently investigated and carefully dismissed the potential social and economic issues in pre-Revolutionary Virginia has concluded, "What remains as the fundamental issue in the coming of the Revolution, then, is nothing more than the contest over constitutional rights."

In a different way Bernard Bailyn in a recent article has clarified and reinforced this revived idealistic interpretation of the Revolution. The accumulative influence of much of the latest historical writing on the character of eighteenth-century American society has led Bailyn to the same insight expressed by Samuel Williams in 1794. What made the Revolution truly revolutionary was not the wholesale disruption of social groups and political institutions, for compared to other revolutions such disruption was slight; rather it was the fundamental alteration in the Americans' structure of values, the way they looked at themselves and their institutions. Bailyn has seized on this basic intellectual shift as a means of explaining the apparent contradiction between the seriousness with which the Americans took their Revolutionary ideas and the absence of radical social and institutional change. The Revolution, argues Bailyn, was not so much the transformation as the realization of American society.

The Americans had been gradually and unwittingly preparing themselves for such a mental revolution since they first came to the New World in the seventeenth century. The substantive changes in American society had taken place in the course of the previous century, slowly, often imperceptibly, as a series of small piecemeal deviations from what was regarded by most Englishmen as the accepted orthodoxy in society, state, and religion. What the Revolution marked, so to speak, was the point when the Americans suddenly blinked and saw their society, its changes, its differences, in a new perspective. Their deviation from European standards, their lack of an established church and a titled aristocracy, their apparent rusticity and general equality, now became desirable, even necessary, elements in the maintenance of their society and politics. The comprehending and justifying, the endowing with high moral purpose, of these confusing and disturbing social and political divergences, Bailyn concludes, was the American Revolution.

Bailyn's more recent investigation of the rich pamphlet literature of the decades before Independence has filled out and refined his idealist interpretation, confirming him in his "rather old-fashioned view that the American Revolution was above all else an ideological-constitutional struggle and not primarily a controversy between social groups undertaken to force changes in the organization of society." While Bailyn's book-length introduction to the first of a multivolumed edition of Revolutionary pamphlets makes no effort to stress the conservative character of the Revolution and indeed emphasizes (in contrast to the earlier article) its radicalism and the dynamic and transforming rather than the rationalizing and declarative quality of Whig thought, it nevertheless represents the culmination of the idealist approach to the history of the Revolution. For "above all else," argues Bailyn, it was the Americans' world-view, the peculiar bundle of notions and beliefs they put together during the imperial debate, "that in the end propelled them into Revolution." Through his study of the Whig pamphlets Bailyn became convinced "that the fear of a comprehensive conspiracy against liberty throughout the English-speaking world—a conspiracy believed to have been nourished in corruption, and of which, it was felt, oppression in America was only the most immediately visible part—lay at the heart of the Revolutionary movement." No one of the various acts and measures of the British government after 1763 could by itself have provoked the extreme and violent response of the American Whigs. But when linked together they formed in the minds of the Americans, imbued with a particular historical understanding of what constituted tyranny, an extensive and frightening program designed to enslave the New World. The Revolution becomes comprehensible only when the mental framework, the Whig world-view into which the Americans fitted the events of the

1760's and 1770's, is known. "It is the development of this view to the point of overwhelming persuasiveness to the majority of American leaders and the meaning this view gave to the events of the time, and not simply an accumulation of grievances," writes Bailyn, "that explains the origins of the American Revolution."

It now seems evident from Bailyn's analysis that it was the Americans' peculiar conception of reality more than anything else that convinced them that tyranny was afoot and that they must fight if their liberty was to survive. By an empathic understanding of a wide range of American thinking Bailyn has been able to offer us a most persuasive argument for the importance of ideas in bringing on the Revolution. Not since Tyler has the intellectual character of the Revolution received such emphasis and never before has it been set out so cogently and completely. It would seem that the idealist explanation of the Revolution has nowhere else to go.

Labeling the recent historical interpretations of the Revolution as "neo-whig" is indeed appropriate, for, as Page Smith has pointed out, "After a century and a half of progress in historical scholarship, in research techniques, in tools and methods, we have found our way to the interpretation held, substantially, by those historians who themselves participated in or lived through the era of, the Revolution." By describing the Revolution as a conservative, principled defense of American freedom against the provocations of the English government, the neo-Whig historians have come full circle to the position of the Revolutionaries themselves and to the interpretation of the first generation of historians. Indeed, as a consequence of this historical atavism, praise for the contemporary or early historians has become increasingly common.

But to say "that the Whig interpretation of the American Revolution may not be as dead as some historians would have us believe" is perhaps less to commend the work of David Ramsay and George Bancroft than to indict the approach of recent historians. However necessary and rewarding the neo-Whig histories have been, they present us with only a partial perspective on the Revolution. The neo-Whig interpretation is intrinsically polemical; however subtly presented, it aims to justify the Revolution. It therefore cannot accommodate a totally different, an opposing, perspective, a Tory view of the Revolution. It is for this reason that the recent publication of Peter Oliver's "Origin and Progress of the American Rebellion" is of major significance, for it offers us—"by attacking the hallowed traditions of the revolution, challenging the motives of the founding fathers, and depicting revolution as passion, plotting, and violence"—an explanation of what happened quite different from what we have been recently accustomed to. Oliver's vivid portrait of the Revolutionaries with his accent on their vicious emotions and interests seriously disturbs the present Whiggish interpretation of the Revolution. It is not that Oliver's description of, say, John Adams as madly ambitious and consumingly resentful is any more correct than Adams's own description of himself as a virtuous and patriotic defender of liberty against tyranny. Both interpretations of Adams are in a sense right, but neither can comprehend the other because each is preoccupied with seemingly contradictory sets of motives. Indeed, it is really these two interpretations that have divided historians of the Revolution ever since.

Any intellectually satisfying explanation of the Revolution must encompass the Tory perspective as well as the Whig, for if we are compelled to take sides and choose between opposing motives—unconscious or avowed, passion or principle, greed or liberty—we will be endlessly caught up in the polemics of the participants themselves. We must, in other words, eventually dissolve the distinction between conscious and unconscious motives, between the Revolutionaries' stated intentions and their supposedly hidden needs and desires, a dissolution that involves somehow relating beliefs and ideas to the social world in which they operate. If we are to understand the causes of the Revolution we must therefore ultimately transcend this problem of motivation. But this we can never do as long as we attempt to explain the Revolution mainly in terms of the intentions of the participants. It is not that men's motives are unimportant; they indeed make events, including revolutions. But the purposes of men, especially in a revolution, are so numerous, so varied, and so contradictory that their complex interaction produces results that no one intended or could even foresee. It is this interaction and these results that recent historians are referring to when they speak so disparagingly of those "underlying determinants" and "impersonal and inexorable forces" bringing on the Revolution. Historical explanation which does not account for these "forces," which, in other words, relies simply on understanding the conscious intentions of the actors, will thus be limited. This preoccupation with men's purposes was what restricted the perspectives of the contemporaneous Whig and Tory interpretations; and it is still the weakness of the neo-Whig histories, and indeed of any interpretation which attempts to explain the events of the Revolution by discovering the calculations from which individuals supposed themselves to have acted. . . .

By implying that certain declared rational purposes are by themselves an adequate explanation for the Americans' revolt, in other words that the Revolution was really nothing more than a contest over constitutional principles, the neo-Whig historians have not only threatened to deny what we have learned of human psychology in the twentieth century, but they have also in fact failed to exploit fully the terms of their own idealist approach by not taking into account all of what the Americans believed and said. Whatever the deficiencies and misunderstandings of the role of ideas in human behavior present in the propagandist studies of the 1930's, these studies did for the first time attempt to deal with the entirety and complexity of American Revolutionary thought—to explain not only all the well-reasoned notions of law and liberty that were so familiar but, more important, all the irrational and hysterical beliefs that had been so long neglected. Indeed, it was the patent absurdity and implausibility of much of what the Americans said that lent credence and persuasiveness to their mistrustful approach to the ideas. Once this exaggerated and fanatical rhetoric was uncovered by the Progressive historians, it should not have subsequently been ignored—no matter how much it may have impugned the reasonableness of the American response. No widely expressed ideas can be dismissed out of hand by the historian.

In his recent analysis of Revolutionary thinking Bernard Bailyn has avoided the neo-Whig tendency to distort the historical reconstruction of the American mind. By comprehending "the assumptions, beliefs, and ideas that lay behind the manifest events of the time," Bailyn has attempted to get inside the Whigs' mind, and to experience vicariously all of what they thought and felt, both their rational constitutional beliefs and their hysterical and emotional ideas as well. The inflammatory phrases, "slavery," "corruption," "conspiracy," that most historians had either ignored or readily dismissed as propaganda, took on a new significance for Bailyn. He came "to suspect that they meant something very real to both the writers and their readers: that there were real fears, real anxieties, a sense of real danger behind these phrases, and not merely the desire to influence by rhetoric and propaganda the inert minds of an otherwise passive populace." No part of American thinking, Bailyn suggests—not the widespread belief in a ministerial conspiracy, not the hostile and vicious indictments of individuals, not the fear of corruption and the hope for regeneration, not any of the violent seemingly absurd distortions and falsifications of what we now believe to be true, in short, none of the frenzied rhetoric—can be safely ignored by the historian seeking to understand the causes of the Revolution.

Bailyn's study, however, represents something other than a more complete and uncorrupted version of the common idealist interpretations of the Revolution. By viewing from the "interior" the Revolutionary pamphlets, which were "to an unusual degree, *explanatory*," revealing "not merely positions taken but the reasons why positions were taken," Bailyn like any idealist historian has sought to discover the motives the participants themselves gave for their actions, to re-enact their thinking at crucial moments, and thereby to recapture some of the "unpredictable reality" of the Revolution. But for Bailyn the very unpredictability of the reality he has disclosed has undermined the idealist obsession with explaining why, in the participants' own estimation, they acted as they did. Ideas emerge as more than explanatory devices, as more than indicators of motives. They become as well objects for analysis in and for themselves, historical events in their own right to be treated as other historical events are treated. Although Bailyn has examined the Revolutionary ideas subjectively from the inside, he has also analyzed them objectively from the outside. Thus, in addition to a contemporary Whig perspective, he presents us with a retrospective view of the ideas—their complexity, their development, and their consequences—that the actual participants did not have. In effect his essay represents what has been called "a Namierism of the history of ideas," a structural analysis of thought that suggests a conclusion about the movement of history not very different from Sir Lewis Namier's, where history becomes something "started in ridiculous beginnings, while small men did things both infinitely smaller and infinitely greater than they knew."

In his *England in the Age of the American Revolution* Namier attacked the Whig tendency to overrate "the importance of the conscious will and purpose in individuals." Above all he urged us "to ascertain and recognize the deeper irrelevancies and incoherence of human actions, which are not so much directed by reason, as invested by it *ex post facto* with the appearances of logic and rationality," to discover the unpredictable reality, where men's motives and intentions were lost in the accumulation and momentum of interacting events. The whole force of Namier's approach tended to squeeze the intellectual content out of what men did. Ideas setting forth principles and purposes for action, said Namier, did not count for much in the movement of history.

In his study of the Revolutionary ideas Bailyn has come to an opposite conclusion: ideas counted for a great deal, not only being responsible for the Revolution but also for transforming the character of American society. Yet in his hands ideas lose that static quality they have commonly had for the Whig historians, the simple statements of intention that so exasperated Namier. For Bailyn the ideas of the Revolutionaries take on an elusive and unmanageable quality, a dynamic self-intensifying character that transcended the intentions and desires of any of the historical participants. By emphasizing how the thought of the colonists was "strangely reshaped, turned in unfamiliar directions," by describing how the Americans "indeliberately, half-knowingly" groped toward "conclusions they could not themselves clearly perceive," by demonstrating how new beliefs and hence new actions were the responses not to desire but to the logic of developing situations, Bailyn has wrested the explanation of the Revolution out of the realm of motivation in which the neo-Whig historians had confined it.

With this kind of approach to ideas, the degree of consistency and devotion to principles become less important, and indeed the major issues of motivation and responsibility over which historians have disagreed become largely irrelevant. Action becomes not the product of rational and conscious calculation but of dimly perceived and rapidly changing thoughts and situations, "where the familiar meaning of ideas and words faded away into confusion, and leaders felt themselves peering into a haze, seeking to bring shifting conceptions somehow into focus." Men become more the victims than the manipulators of their ideas, as their thought unfolds in ways few anticipated, "rapid, irreversible, and irresistible," creating new problems, new considerations, new ideas, which have their own unforeseen implications. In this kind of atmosphere the Revolution, not at first desired by the Americans, takes on something of an inevitable character, moving through a process of escalation into levels few had intended or perceived. It no longer makes sense to assign motives or responsibility to particular individuals for the totality of what happened. Men were involved in a complicated web of phenomena, ideas, and situations, from which in retrospect escape seems impossible.

By seeking to uncover the motives of the Americans expressed in the Revolutionary pamphlets, Bailyn has ended by demonstrating the autonomy of ideas as phenomena, where the ideas operate, as it were, over the heads of the participants, taking them in directions no one could have foreseen. His discussion of Revolutionary thought thus represents a move back to a deterministic approach to the Revolution, a determinism, however, which is different from that which the neo-Whig historians have so recently and self-consciously abandoned. Yet while the suggested determinism is thoroughly idealist—indeed never before has the force of ideas in bringing on the Revolution been so emphatically put—its implications are not. By helping to purge our writing about the Revolution of its concentration on constitutional principles and its stifling judicial-like pre-occupation with motivation and responsibility, the study serves to open the way for new questions and new appraisals. In fact, it is out of the very completeness of his idealist interpreta-tion, out of his exposition of the extraordinary nature—the very dynamism and emotionalism—of the Americans' thought that we have the evidence for an entirely different, a behaviorist, perspective on the causes of the American Revolution. Bailyn's book-length introduction to his edition of Revolutionary pam-phlets is therefore not only a point of fulfillment for the idealist approach to the Revolution, it is also a point of departure for a new look at the social sources of the Revolution.

It seems clear that historians of eighteenth-century America and the Revolution cannot ignore the force of ideas in history to the extent that Namier and his students have done in their investigations of eighteenth-century English politics. This is not to say, however, that the Namier approach to English politics has been crucially limiting and distorting. Rather it may suggest that the Namier denigration of ideas and principles is inap-plicable for American politics because the American social situation in which ideas operated was very different from that of eighteenth-century England. It may be that ideas are less meaningful to a people in a socially stable situation. Only when ideas have become stereotyped reflexes do evasion and hypocrisy and the Namier mistrust of what men believe become significant. Only in a relatively settled society does ideology become a kind of habit, a bundle of widely shared and instinctive conventions, offering ready-made explanations for men who are not being compelled to ask any serious questions. Conversely, it is perhaps only in a relatively unsettled, disordered society, where the questions come faster than men's answers, that ideas become truly vital and creative.

Paradoxically it may be the very vitality of the Americans' ideas, then, that suggests the need to examine the circumstances in which they flourished. Since ideas and beliefs are ways of perceiving and explaining the world, the nature of the ideas expressed is determined as much by the character of the world being confronted as by the internal development of inherited and borrowed conceptions. Out of the multitude of inherited and transmitted ideas available in the eighteenth century, Americans selected and emphasized those which seemed to make meaningful what was happening to them. In the colonists' use of classical literature, for example, "their detailed knowledge and engaged interest covered only one era and one small group of writers," Plutarch, Livy, Cicero, Sallust, and Tacitus— those who "had hated and feared the trends of their own time, and in their writing had contrasted the present with a better past, which they endowed with qualities absent from their own, corrupt era." There was always, in Max Weber's term, some sort of elective affinity between the Americans' interests and their beliefs, and without that affinity their ideas would not have possessed the peculiar character and persuasiveness they did. Only the most revolutionary social needs and circumstances could have sustained such revolutionary ideas.

When the ideas of the Americans are examined comprehensively, when all of the Whig rhetoric, irrational as well as rational, is taken into account, one cannot but be struck by the predominant characteristics of fear and frenzy, the exaggerations and the enthusiasm, the general sense of social corruption and disorder out of which would be born a new world of benevolence and harmony where Americans would become the "eminent examples of every divine and social virtue." As Bailyn and the propaganda studies have amply shown, there is simply too much fanatical and millennial thinking even by the best minds that must be explained before we can characterize the Americans' ideas as peculiarly rational and legalistic and thus view the Revolution as merely a conservative defense of constitutional liberties. To isolate refined and nicely-reasoned arguments from the writings of John Adams and Jefferson is not only to disregard the more inflamed expressions of the rest of the Whigs but also to overlook the enthusiastic extravagance —the paranoiac obsession with a diabolical Crown conspiracy and the dream of a restored Saxon era—in the thinking of Adams and Jefferson themselves.

The ideas of the Americans seem, in fact, to form what can only be called a revolutionary syndrome. If we were to confine ourselves to examining the Revolutionary rhetoric alone, apart from what happened politically or socially, it would be virtually impossible to distinguish the American Revolution from any other revolution in modern Western history. In the kinds of ideas expressed the American Revolution is remarkably similar to the seventeenth-century Puritan Revolution and to the eighteenth-century French Revolution: the same general disgust with a chaotic and corrupt world, the same anxious and angry bombast, the same excited fears of conspiracies by depraved men, the same utopian hopes for the construction of a new and virtuous order. It was not that this syndrome of ideas was simply transmitted from one generation or from one people to another. It was rather perhaps that similar, though hardly identical, social situations called forth within the limitations of inherited and available conceptions similar modes of expression. Although we need to know much more about the sociology of revolutions and collective movements, it does seem possible that particular patterns of thought, particular forms of expression, correspond to certain basic social experiences. There may be, in other words, typical modes of expression, typical kinds of beliefs and values, characterizing a revolutionary situation, at least within roughly similar Western societies. Indeed, the types of ideas manifested may be the best way of identifying a collective movement as a revolution. As one student of revolutions writes, "It is on the basis of a knowledge of men's beliefs that we can distinguish their behaviour from riot, rebellion or insanity."

It is thus the very nature of the Americans' rhetoric—its obsession with corruption and disorder, its hostile and conspiratorial outlook, and its millennial vision of a regenerated society—that reveals as nothing else apparently can the American Revolution as a true revolution with its sources lying deep in the social structure. For this kind of frenzied rhetoric could spring only from the most severe sorts of social strain. The grandiose and feverish language of the Americans was indeed the natural, even the inevitable, expression of a people caught up in a revolutionary situation, deeply alienated from the existing sources of authority and vehemently involved in a basic reconstruction of their political and social order. The hysteria of the Americans' thinking was but a measure of the intensity of their revolutionary passions. Undoubtedly the growing American alienation from British authority contributed greatly to this revolutionary situation. Yet the very weakness of the British imperial system and the accumulating ferocity of American antagonism to it suggests that other sources of social strain were being fed into the revolutionary movement. It may be that the Progressive historians in their preoccupation with internal social problems were more right than we have recently been willing to grant. It would be repeating their mistake, however, to expect this internal social strain necessarily to take the form of coherent class conflict or overt social disruption. The sources of revolutionary social stress may have been much more subtle but no less severe. . . .

It is through the Whigs' ideas, then, that we may be led back to take up where the Progressive historians left off in their investigation of the internal social sources of the Revolution. By working through the ideas—by reading them imaginatively and relating them to the objective social world they both reflected and confronted—we may be able to eliminate the unrewarding distinction between conscious and unconscious motives, and eventually thereby to combine a Whig with a Tory, an idealist with a behaviorist, interpretation. For the ideas, the rhetoric, of the Americans was never obscuring but remarkably revealing of their deepest interests and passions. What they expressed may not have been for the most part factually true, but it was always psychologically true. In this sense their rhetoric was never detached from the social and political reality; and indeed it becomes the best entry into an understanding of that reality. Their repeated overstatements of reality, their incessant talk of "tyranny" when there seems to have been no real oppression, their obsession with "virtue," "luxury," and "corruption," their devotion to "liberty" and "equality"—all these notions were neither manipulated propaganda nor borrowed empty abstractions, but ideas with real personal and social significance for those who used them. Propaganda could never move men to revolution. No popular leader, as John Adams put it, has ever been able "to persuade a large people, for any length of time together, to think themselved wronged, injured, and oppressed, unless they really were, and saw and felt it to be so." The ideas had relevance; the sense of oppression and injury, although often displaced onto the imperial system, was nonetheless real. It was indeed the meaningfulness of the connection between what the Americans said and what they felt that gave the ideas their propulsive force and their overwhelming persuasiveness.

It is precisely the remarkable revolutionary character of the Americans' ideas now being revealed by historians that best indicates that something profoundly unsettling was going on in the society, that raises the question, as it did for the Progressive historians, why the Americans should have expressed such thoughts. With their crude conception of propaganda the Progressive historians at least attempted to grapple with the problem. Since we cannot regard the ideas of the Revolutionaries as simply propaganda, the question still remains to be answered. "When 'ideas' in full cry drive past," wrote Arthur F. Bentley in his classic behavioral study, *The Process of Government,* "the thing to do with them is to accept them as an indication that something is happening; and then search carefully to find out what it really is they stand for, what the factors of the social life are that are expressing themselves through the ideas." Precisely because they sought to understand both the Revolutionary ideas and American society, the behaviorist historians of the Progressive generation, for all of their crude conceptualizations, their obsession with "class" and hidden economic interests, and their treatment of ideas as propaganda, have still offered us an explanation of the Revolutionary era so powerful and so comprehensive that no purely intellectual interpretation will ever replace it.

13

Benjamin Quarles
"The shortage of manpower soon caused a change of heart"

Until recently only a few historians engaged in research on the role of black men in American history. Much of the work that had been done concerned itself with the institution of slavery. That the last twenty years has seen a greatly increased interest in Negro history is largely a by-product of the civil rights struggles that have developed since World War II. Not only have many more historians made American Negro history a chosen field of research but publications on the subject have found a larger market. Although no new interpretation of the American Revolution has resulted, such studies do contribute to a fuller understanding of that movement. The mere existence of this new interest and these new researches provide an excellent example of how historians can serve as mediators between an ever-changing "present" and the past.

In the following passage Benjamin A. Quarles, who is at Morgan State College in Baltimore, provides a resumé of his study of black Americans during the Revolution.

The American Revolution touched all classes in society, even Negroes. On the eve of the conflict, the same religious and polit-

SOURCE. Benjamin Quarles, *The Negro in the American Revolution.* Chapel Hill: University of North Carolina Press for the Institute of Early American History and Culture, 1961, pp. 197–200. Reprinted by permission of publisher and author.

ical idealism that stirred the resistance to Britain deepened the sentiment against slavery. The memorable phrases of the Declaration of Independence which asserted the equality of man set forth a principle which could never be wholly reconciled with the existence of slavery. During the war itself, the abolition movement bore its first fruits, and within two decades after the war's end, all the Northern states were emancipating their slaves.

The actual fighting presented more immediate opportunities for obtaining freedom. Britain and America both needed black manpower, and both were prepared to give the Negro the freedom he sought. Since liberating the slaves of American rebels cost her nothing and at the same time hampered the patriot war effort, Britain was first to make the offer. Lord Dunmore, at bay in Virginia during the opening months of the yet undeclared war, initiated the practice of inviting slaves to desert their American masters. Although Dunmore was soon driven from the Old Dominion, the number of Negroes who tried to join his forces disclosed the readiness of slaves to seek freedom within the British lines. Henceforth, solicitation of Negroes became a key factor in British policy.

On the American side, free Negroes served in the military and naval forces from the beginning of the war, but the enlistment of slaves raised so many difficulties and aroused such opposition, particularly in the South, that it was at first avoided. The need to counteract British appeals and the shortage of manpower soon caused a change of heart. Congress and most of the states north of the Potomac endorsed a policy of recruiting slaves for military duty, granting freedom as the reward for faithful service.

As an American soldier, the Negro proved to be much like his fellows. His morale was likely to be above average—military service was a step up in life for him, and active campaigning was often no more arduous and certainly more exciting than the routine of the plantation. With little investment in a civilian existence or occupation, Negroes were suitable recruits for the Continental army, which Congress desired to enlist on the basis of three years or the duration of the war. Serving in racially mixed units, the Negro did not stand out distinctly; his military personality blended into the composite portrait of the undistinguished but indispensable foot solider.

Negroes also served in state forces, particularly in the North. In the plantation areas of the South, the heavy slave population made it seem a risky venture to employ slaves as soldiers, moreover inducting them into the army took them away from the tobacco or rice fields, where their labor was of paramount importance. The plantation states all took a few free Negroes into their armed forces, and Maryland provided for the enlistment of slaves. Georgia and the Carolinas were never willing to take this last step, and resisted it to the end.

Service at sea offered a better field of opportunity for Negroes; even in the South there was less reluctance to employ them aboard ship than as soldiers. The Continental navy welcomed black recruits, especially free Negro sailors from New England coastal towns. Generally, however, the Continental service was outbid by the state navies: Massachusetts and Connecticut took all the Negroes they could get for maritime service. Among Southern states, Virginia was most inclined to use black seamen, enlisting nearly 150 during the war. The highest function open to Southern Negro sailors was to act as pilots in local waters, and several attained considerable reputation for their diligence and success. Apart from duty in regular maritime forces, Negroes went to sea on privateers. As the captains of these private ships of war seldom bothered to inquire into the status of the black members of their crews, many runaway slaves thus found sanctuary.

Individuals who bore arms or served on ships or who took advantage of opportunities to act as spies, guides, or informers stand out from the general mass of the Negro population whose contribution to the American cause was anonymous labor. Negroes erected fortifications, manufactured cannon and gun carriages, worked in the salt and lead mines, repaired roads, and drove wagons. To procure Negro labor, state governments and Continental military officers resorted to a variety of techniques: impressing, hiring, or purchasing slaves. Whatever the method, it never yielded a sufficient supply to meet the need.

The military potential represented by America's large Negro population was available to the British in the regions they occupied or controlled. In the South, some hundreds of runaway slaves were converted into shock troops, but the British needed blacks less as soldiers than as military laborers. Thousands of Negro carpenters, hostlers, axemen, miners, and blacksmiths increased the striking power of the British forces. Unable to get enough slaves for their purposes, many British commanders induced free Negroes to take employment, paying them 2s. or 3s. a day as smiths, sawyers, armorers, and turnwheelers. Unskilled Negroes were often sent out on foraging parties to run off the livestock of American patriots and strip their fields, barns, and cellars.

Since slaves were property, they constituted a source of wealth which both the British and the Americans exploited for a variety of purposes. Southern state governments used them to pay official salaries, enlistment bounties, and back-pay due to the troops. To Americans as well as the British, the slaves of the enemy were legitimate spoils of war, which not only provided booty but deprived the enemy of vital resources. In the South, especially in the later stages of the conflict, slave-raiding was one of the primary objects of war.

When the British evacuated American ports, they took with them most of the Negroes who had come into their lines. Alert to this possibility, which entailed immense loss of property to Americans, General Washington personally presented the American case to Sir Guy Carleton, the British commander-in-chief. Joint commissions were set up to supervise the evacuation, but they were of little help to Americans in recovering slaves. The British never yielded in their contention that the terms of the peace treaty did not cover Negroes who accepted British protection before the preliminary articles of peace were signed. Irate Americans could only fume as their former slaves were evacuated. Their losses gave rise to a diplomatic issue that plagued Anglo-American relations for a quarter of a century.

Negroes who went with the British were shipped to the West Indies, Canada, England, and Continental Europe. Those owned by loyalists or British subjects remained slaves, of course, and merely followed their masters. Others who had achieved freedom by embracing the British side in the Revolution often failed to improve their lot significantly. Some, in fact, were forced back to slavery; in other instances, they had difficulty in obtaining the land grants which had been promised them. In Nova Scotia, a group of disillusioned Negroes numbering nearly twelve hundred, obtained permission from the Sierra Leone Company in 1792 to settle on its territory in West Africa.

Negroes who remained in America likewise found the postwar period a disappointment to their hopes. The condition of slaves on the plantations was unchanged. Nevertheless, the Negro had made some gains. Many slaves had become free, and some free Negroes had improved their status. The emancipation movement was gaining strength in the North. Ultimately, the colored people of America benefited from the irreversible commitment of the new nation to the principles of liberty and equality.

14   *Jesse Lemisch*

"The history of the powerless, the inarticulate, the poor has not yet begun to be written"

The depth and extent of American racism during the civil rights struggles, the tragic persistence of poverty and hunger in an "Age of Affluence," and the sharp conflict over American intervention in Vietnam have focused attention during the 1960's on divergence rather than agreement. It was natural that some historians should begin to question the existence of the American consensus of the neo-Whig scholars. Had not class struggles perhaps existed throughout American history? Although it is too early to determine whether a "New Left" interpretation of the American Revolution will develop, such students of the subject as Staughton Lynd and Jesse Lemisch are already posing new questions and offering new emphases.

Jesse Lemisch believes that historians have misunderstood the inarticulate poor and weak of the Revolutionary era. The latter were not, as Arthur M. Schlesinger, Sr., once described them, men whose "brains were in their biceps." Nor were they merely the tools of scheming politicians, manipulated for purposes beyond their understanding. Rather, the lower classes had real grievances against the British and real goals in fighting them.

SOURCE. Jesse Lemisch, "The American Revolution Seen from the Bottom Up," in *Towards a New Past: Dissenting Essays in American History,* ed. by Barton J. Bernstein (New York: Random House 1968), pp. 3-6, 12-27, 29. Reprinted by permission of Pantheon Books, Division of Random House, Inc., and the author.

In 1921 Samuel Eliot Morison used what he called a "blue-book of Boston provincial society" to demonstrate the ethnic diversity of the "Yankee race," and measured the growth of towns around Boston by the construction of mansions. Morison admired the "codfish aristocracy," and he looked at colonial Massachusetts largely from their point of view. Thus he imposed on the entire society the characteristics and values which he had discovered in an admiring examination of a part of it: the characteristics of the "Yankee race" seemed identical to those of the "middle class."

In the half-century since, historians have become more sophisticated in their generalizations. In a landmark essay in the fifties one of them criticized his colleagues for their failure "to think or write as social scientists" and especially for their "reliance on leaders" as a basis for describing a "class, section, or society as a whole." But then he proceeded to urge the assembling of "the large number of career lines of different types of social *leaders* [emphasis added], essential for a picture of who succeeded in the society and how" and offered the reader a paean to the entrepreneur and a plea for more histories of business and of "important business figures." Instead of replacing elite history with a history of "average people," he had merely traded in the heroes of politics for the heroes of business.

Despite our pretensions to social science, we would seem to be hardly more genuinely scientific than we were fifty years ago. Many social scientists continue to draw conclusions about entire societies on the basis of examinations of the minority at the top. This approach has distorted our view and, sometimes, cut us off from past reality. Our earliest history has been seen as a period of consensus and classlessness, in part because our historians have chosen to see it that way. One of them, describing colonial Massachusetts as a "middle-class democracy," has tried to show that urban workers could qualify for the vote by offering evidence which sometimes proves only that their *employers* could do so, much as one might demonstrate that slaves had it easy by describing the life of the antebellum Southern belle. Another has diluted a useful study of Loyalism and blocked our understanding of any possible class aspects of this phenomenon by presenting his data in a form which does not distinguish between employers and employees. In a valuable study of legislatures before and after the Revolution, another tells us that "colonials . . . did not yet conceive that the *demos* should actually govern." *Which* colonials? Earlier in the same article he had noted that "the majority . . . were not asked, and as they were unable to speak or write on the subject, their opinions were uncertain." Thus the conclusion about "colonials" indicates either that the historian has allowed the opinions of an elite to stand for those of a majority or that he has forgotten that he really does not know what the majority thought. This dilemma suggests two very different ways of writing history.

The first way, the one criticized so far, assumes the absence of conflict without demonstrating it. After consensus has been assumed, the very categories of analysis foreclose the possibility that the researcher will find evidence of conflict. History of this sort can lead, as Staughton Lynd has noted, to such grotesqueries as the claim that "equality" is at the center of American history, a claim which ignores the Negro, among others. (One might with as much evidence claim that the main theme of American history has been a kind of righteous hypocrisy and point to the gap between pretension and performance indicated in our early history by slaveowners discoursing on equality and, more recently, in the newspeak of a nation which claims to value justice above all but defines justice as order and values power more than either.) In a world in which many non-American movie audiences cheer every time another cowboy hits the dust we can no longer afford such obtuseness. And in our history we can no longer allow the powerful to speak for the poweless.

Those who rule may have, as Barrington Moore has put it, "the most to hide about the way society works." And these are the very people who are most favored by history and historical sources. Thus "sympathy with the victims of historical processes and skepticism about the victors' claims provide essential safeguards against being taken in by the dominant mythology." (Indeed, Herbert Marcuse has suggested, in defense of Lord Acton's moralism, that a society may be most accurately judged through an examination of its worst injustices:

such an approach uncovers "the deepest layer of the whole system, the structure which holds it together, the essential condition for the efficiency of its political and economic organization.") This sympathy for the powerless brings us closer to objectivity; in practice, it leads the historian to describe past societies as they appeared from the bottom rather than the top, more from the point of view of the inarticulate than of the articulate. . . .

During the period of the American Revolution . . . the powerless refused to stay in the places to which a theory of deference and subordination assigned them. Among the most blatant cases are those of Negroes who petitioned for that freedom to which, *"as men,"* they claimed they had "a naturel [sic] right"; they reminded their masters that their struggle was merely "[In imitat]ion of the Lawdable [sic] Example of the Good People of these States" who were "nobly contending, in the Cause of Liberty," and lectured them on "the inconsistancey [sic] of acting themselves the part which they condem [sic] and oppose in others." Merrill Jensen has ably described the pursuit of expanded political power by disfranchised whites and has presented clear evidence of conflict bwteen [sic] rich and poor. Staughton Lynd has seen "government-from-below" in the conduct and "ideology" of New York's mechanics on the eve of the Revolution. In 1774 Gouverneur Morris observed New York's "mob" beginning "to think and to reason," debating with the rich on whether government should henceforth be "aristocratic or democratic." In 1776 much of the impetus for the movement to overthrow Pennsylvania's old government and draw up a new constitution came from below, in mass meetings and in the activities of privates in the militia.

Insofar as activities such as these focused on questions of voting, they reflect a striking failure of the lower class to provide the deference which their rulers expected of them. John Adams might boast of the respect of the Massachusetts electorate for what he later called the "natural aristocracy," and later writers might assure us that colonials did not suppose that they should govern: according to Tom Paine, voters too poor to vote would borrow or lie their way up to the property qualifications and they would do it without hesitation. Let John Adams boast about the freeness of elections in Massachusetts: in 1770 Philadelphia mechanics would refuse to rubberstamp tickets set in advance by "leading men," while their brothers in New York would rebel against the coercions which *made* them vote, again and again, for the same families:

"Many of the poorer People having deeply felt the Aristocratic Power or rather, the intollerable Tyranny of the great and opulent, who (such is the shocking Depravity of the Times, and their utter Contempt of all public Virtue and Patriotism) have openly threatened them with the Loss of their Employment, and to arrest them for Debt, unless they gave their Voices as they were directed. . . . [Because of the] exorbitant Influence of the Rich over the Poor, . . . [we] need . . . a secret Method of voting."

If deference ever existed, it was clearly gone when Americans began to describe the supporters of open balloting as "the great and the mighty, and the rich, and the long Wiggs and the Squaretoes, and all Manner of Wickednesses in high places."

"In Pursuance of the Declaration for Independency . . . ," and within less than a week, New York's debtors had been released from prison. The freeing of these "oppressed" indicates that some took their egalitarianism literally and extended their literalism to economics: Paine and Woolman were not alone in identifying economic subordination with lack of freedom. Ever since Thomas Morton's "partners and consociates" had rejected servitude in Virginia to "live together as equals" amidst the pleasures of Merrymount, many Americans had made the same identification and chosen freedom. *"I am Flesh and Blood, as well as my Master,"* said a servant who had murdered him, *"and therefore I know no Reason, why my Master should not obey me, as well as I obey him."* Bound servants conspired to run away, to strike and to rebel, aiming "either [to] be free or dye for it," and crying out for those *"who would be for liberty and freed from bondage"* to join them. Slaves, too, displayed what Cotton Mather called "a *Fondness* for *Freedom*": they revolted, ran away, and governed themselves in runaway communities from which they launched attacks against their former masters; they fought for "Liberty & Life" and marched "with Colours displayed, and . . . Drums beating"—a black Spirit of '76. And long before the first trade unions, free white workers had engaged in strikes, slowdowns, and other protests, in some cases directly opposing laws which punished them for disobedience. "Mutiny" is a poor word to describe those seamen who seized their ship, renamed it *Liberty,* and chose their course and a new captain by voting. Many colonial laborers, white and Negro alike, expressed their refusal to defer by protests in which the economic grievance is hardly distinguishable from the social and political.

"Colonials" meant many people, often people in conflict with one another: there was, from the very beginning, something of a struggle over who should rule at home. The people on the bottom of that conflict were also involved in the struggle for home rule, but their activities have been made to seem an extension of the conduct of the more articulate, who have been seen as their manipulators. The inarticulate could act on their own, and often for very sound reasons. It is time that we examined the coming of the American Revolution from their perspective. What follows is an attempt to sketch some of the kinds of events and considerations which should be explored if we are to understand what opposition to the British meant to those who were to bear the burden of the fighting and dying.

Late in October of 1765 the Stamp Act Congress added its Declarations to those of the individual colonies: the Act was unconstitutional. As Edmund and Helen Morgan have put it, "it would have been difficult to find an American anywhere who did not believe in them [Declarations of the Stamp Act Congress]—as far as they went." The problem was that many Americans did not think that they went far enough, "did not choose that it should ever once be thought that the Enjoyment of their Rights depended merely upon the Success of these Representations or the Courtesy of those to whom they were made."

The Stamp Act Congress had adjourned without answering the question, What is to be *done?* The Stamp Act riots showed that the mob had begun to think and reason. Historians have been hesitant to acknowledge it. Instead they have preferred to accept the testimony of British officials who attributed the riots to "the Wiser and better Sort," who stirred up the lower class in behalf of a cause in which that class had no real interest; thus they easily turned to plunder and violence for its own sake. But gentlemen of property associated themselves with mob violence only under the most extreme conditions. Those conditions had not been achieved in 1765. British officials assumed that the lawyers and property owners were the riots' secret leaders partly because of a bias which said that leaders *had* to be people of "Consequence." In addition, these officials were accustomed to confronting members of the upper class as political adversaries in the courts and in the assembly halls. But a new politics—a politics of the street—was replacing the old politics—the politics of the assembly hall. British officials failed to understand these new politics. Wherever they went—and most of them did not go very far—they saw lawyers, merchants, and men of substance. When events which displeased them took place in the streets, they understood them only in their limited frame of reference. Transferring events to that frame, they saw only their old enemies.

The upper classes may not have been pulling the strings in the Stamp Act riots. The assumption that an uninterested mob had to be artificially aroused—created—disregards the ability of the people to think for themselves; like everyone else in the colonies, they had real grievances against the British. Unlike others, they had fewer legal channels through which to express their grievances. So they took to the streets in pursuit of political goals. Within that context, their "riots" were really extremely orderly and expressed a clear purpose. Again and again, when the mob's leaders lost control, the mob went on to attack the logical political enemy, not to plunder. They were led but not manipulated: to dismantle the puppet show is not to do away with the whole concept of leadership, but instead of cynical fomentors, we find direction of the most rudimentary sort, a question of setting times, of priorities, and in the heat of the riot, of getting from one street to another in the quickest way possible.

The struggle against the Stamp Act was also a struggle against colonial leadership. Declarations had not prevented the Act's taking effect. Those who had *declared* now had to *do,* but they could do no better than a boycott: the cessation of all business which required the use of stamps. This strategy put pressure on the English merchants, but it also increased the pressure on the American poor, the hungry, the prisoners in city jails who could not hope for release so long as the lawyers refused to do business.

Radicals protested against the absurdity of American blustering about liberty and then refusing to do anything about it: if the law was wrong, then it was no law and business ought to go on as usual without the use of stamps. They urged disobedience. Upper-class leaders demanded legality and tried, sometimes by shady means, to suppress or distort this dissent. But the radicals continued their pressure, and they were supported by the self-defeating character of the boycott strategy. The more time that passed without ship sailings, the more attractive a policy of disobedience became to merchants, and they began to send their ships out without stamped papers. British officials began to cave in: they were worried about "an Insurrection of the Poor against the Rich," united action by unemployed artisans and the increasing numbers of unruly seamen who were pouring into the colonial cities and finding no way to get out. The seamen—"the . . . people . . . most dangerous on these Occasions" —especially worried customs officials; instead of waiting for them to force their captains to sail without stamps, the officials yielded, giving way before enormous pressures and allowing a radical triumph. Then the Parliament itself backed down, repealing the Stamp Act. The poor people of the colonies had reason to congratulate themselves: word of their actions had thrown a scare into Parliament, and they might even suspect that the economic rationale which Parliament offered for repeal covered its fear of a challenge not so much to its view of the constitution as to its actual authority in the colonies. Thus the meaning of the Stamp Act crisis goes beyond the pursuit of constitutional principles. The lower class had spoken out against the British, against deference, and against colonial leadership, and they had won.

The repeal of the Stamp Act left the Sugar Act of 1764 still on the books, and in 1767 Parliament added a new revenue act. Oliver M. Dickerson has described the activities of the new American Board of Customs Commissioners in enforcing these acts beginning in 1768 as "customs racketeering" and has blamed the Board for transforming "thousands of loyal British subjects into active revolutionists." Corrupt customs officers made seizures on technicalities and pocketed the proceeds. The Hancocks and the Laurenses suffered greatly, but the poor suffered more. Even the pettiest of woodboats in purely local trade were seized; even the common seaman had his chest rifled and its contents confiscated. Seamen, small traders, and rich merchants all came to identify British authority with corruption and injustice.

Customs racketeering was on the wane by mid-1770. This was due in large part to popular opposition and especially to the withdrawal of troops from Boston: the Commissioners could not survive without armed support. The troops left Boston after the street fight which came to be known as the Boston Massacre. The Massacre, in turn, grew out of an antagonism between the troops and the population which has been given too little attention. Long-standing practice in the British army allowed off-duty soldiers to take civilian employment, and they did so at wages which undercut those given to American workingmen: soldiers in New York in 1770 worked for between 37.5 per cent and 50 per cent of the wages offered to Americans for the same work. As might be expected, this situation led to great antagonisms, especially in hard times. In Boston, a British soldier looking for work in a ropewalk in 1770 was told by one of the employees to "go and clean my s[hi]t house." The insult led to a fistfight, which led to an armed attack by more soldiers; the soldiers were defeated and humiliated and vowed to take their revenge. On the evening of March 5 one of the ropemakers who had been wounded in the earlier encounter led a mob which took on the rampaging soldiers. "Come on you rascals, you bloody backs, you lobster scoundrels, fire if you dare, G[o] damn you, fire and be dammed, we know you dare not." Somebody did dare: when the smoke cleared, the ropemaker was dead along with two others and several wounded (of whom two would later die).

The Boston Massacre was widely and rapidly publicized throughout the colonies, but it is only the best known of several such incidents. The Battle of Golden Hill, which had arisen from similar causes, left one New Yorker dead and several cruelly injured in two days of battle with the soldiers six weeks before. This was the culmination of years of antagonism. The Sons of Liberty erected Liberty Poles; the soldiers tore them down. Ostentatiously armed soldiers paraded the streets, drums and bugles assaulted the ears. The people tried to silence them, to disarm them, to run them out of town. A governor noticed the "coldness and distance" between the people and the military. Conflict between classes developed as antagonism directed itself at those employers who hired off-duty soldiers. The people were tired of paying a poor tax to maintain the soldiers' "Whores and Bastards." Gangs of seamen patrolled the docks with clubs and drove away soldiers, promising to take vengeance on those who hired them.

Just as in the Stamp Act riots, the official theory blamed the Battle of Golden Hill on manipulation. And once again, in New York as in Boston, the mob had adequate reason to act on its own. An unfriendly observer who mistakenly saw mere political opportunism in the slogans of the sixties and seventies nonetheless saw the unity of American popular grievances:

"... may it not from what has happened, be justly suspected, that the frequent Notices to meet at *Liberty* Poll [sic], the violent Rage and Resentment which *some* People have endeavoured generally to excite against Soldiers, pretended to proceed from a Love of Liberty, and a Regard to the *Interests* of the Poor; do all tend to the same End, although the Pretences have been so very different.—May not,—No Money to the Troops,—whoraw for [secret] Ballotting,—employ no Soldiers—all mean the same Thing?—Liberty is the Pretext. ..."

Economic and political deprivation were one and the same,

and the people opposed the deprivers whether they were Englishmen or Americans.

The British Navy was as unpopular in the colonies as was the Army. One of the reasons for the Navy's unpopularity has been almost entirely missed by historians who have shown too little concern for those matters which concern the inarticulate. Impressment, previously seen as significant only in connection with the War of 1812, also played a role in bringing on the Revolution. Although the poor were the press gang's peculiar victims, all classes suffered by the practice. "Kiss my arse, you dog," shouted the captain to the merchants as he made off with their men: their numbers mounted into the tens of thousands. The complaints of American governmental bodies spoke for the merchant, not the seaman; they focused on the harmful effects of the practice on colonial trade and seemed almost as critical of those who violently resisted as of the Royal Navy. So the seamen and poor people of the colonies were on their own. Historians have failed to see the significance of their active opposition to impressment: one seems to put blame on seamen for escaping and fighting back, much as one might blame slaves for the same offenses; another, admitting that colonial crowds became "political" in 1765, sees the innumerable impressment riots before that date as "ideologically inert." But the seamen were fighting, literally, for their life, liberty, and property, and their violence was all the politics they could have. Mostly they were inarticulate, and we must read their purpose in their actions; sometimes one would leave us with words linking his thoughts to his conduct:

"I know who you are. You are the lieutenant of a man-of-war, come with a press-gang to deprive me of my liberty. You have no right to impress me. I have retreated from you as far as I can ... I and my companions are determined to stand upon our defense. Stand off."

Impressment, both at sea and ashore, brought bloodshed throughout the colonial period: how much we will never know, for it is in the nature of impressment that much of it went unrecorded both in ships' logs and in sources on shore. How do generalizations about "salutary neglect" stand up when viewed thus, from the bottom? And how much more comprehensible is the violence of the urban mob in the sixties and seventies in the light of previous and continued impressment. All of this bloodshed and violence was not irrelevant to the Revolution. The legalists who were to lead that Revolution were sensitive to the fact that much of this impressment was illegal under British law and inconsistent with "the Natural Rights of Mankind." The men who fought in that Revolution did so, in part, because of an ancient tradition of violent resistance to British tyranny. Feelings were so deep that almost four decades later an enduring folk memory of oppression by the same "haughty, cruel, and gasconading nation" would help to drive the American people to war again. . . .

Who threw the tea in Boston Harbor remains very much a mystery to this day. A merchant speculated the next day that the Tea Party was conducted so efficiently that there must have been "People of sense and more discernment than the vulgar among the Actors." This is hardly evidence, but a recent account accepts it unquestioningly and consistently speculates in the direction of manipulation and elite control when evidence is unavailable. But certainly there is nothing beyond the most uneducated man's capacity in the events of that December night in 1773: that the mob showed up with lanterns and hatchets, attached block and tackle to the chests, raised them from the holds, and emptied the tea in the harbor seems more nearly to suggest the skills of the lower class than to be evidence of an operation so clever as to be explicable only by upper-class manipulation. We do not know who did it, and we need to take a fresh look.

Excessive attention to *Common Sense* for its propaganda values has obscured its substantive meaning as an expression of populist democracy. Indeed, the very concept of "propaganda" has perhaps hindered us more than it has helped us to understand the causes of the American Revolution. "We know today," wrote Philip Davidson in 1941, "that large bodies of people never cooperate in any complex movement except under the guidance of a central machine operated by a comparatively few people.

. . ." Davidson found a few people—men like Tom Paine and Sam Adams—managing such a campaign: " 'By their fruits ye shall know them.' " The assumption here is that one can read back from the "fruits"—the Revolution—to the efforts of propagandists, that is, that Paine and Adams in some sense *caused* the Revolution. Sam Adams' biographer called his subject " 'Dictator' of Boston," "keeper" of a "trained mob," the "Pioneer in Propaganda" who "deliberately set out to provoke crises that would lead to the separation of mother country and colonies." Similarly, David Hawke has seen the coming of revolution in Pennsylvania as the outcome of efforts by "a small band of men" who staged mass meetings and used propaganda and other devious methods. All of this smacks of unproved conspiracy and utterly ignores the fact that Paine did speak "common sense": the Revolution has substantive causes and is rooted in genuine grievances; to explain it as the result of efficient propaganda is to belittle the reality of the grievances and to suggest that the Americans were largely content until they were aroused by a few demagogues.

The final test of the agency of the lower class is their conduct in the Revolution: if they had been tricked into rebellion by demagoguery and propaganda, we might expect them to have had second thoughts when the fighting became bloody. From April 19, 1775, the war was fought, on the American side, by a people in arms, understanding and interpreting their war goals in their own way. The American technique was frequently that of guerrilla warfare, depending on mobility, withdrawal, and unexpected counterattack: they fled when they could not win and turned and fought only when they had a good chance of victory. The Revolution was like modern guerrilla wars in another sense. In guerrilla warfare, according to the aphorism, the people are the water and the troops are the fish who inhabit that water. The troops must live off the people, retaining their support not by coercion but rather because the people believe in and support the cause for which the troops fight. Although the analogy with guerrilla warfare is only an analogy, it is suggestive. As long as the Americans continued to fight, it was impossible for the British to win the war. Mere military conquest was insignificant: to win, the British would have had to occupy simultaneously the entire populated area of the thirteen colonies, and even then their victory would have been unstable, a peace maintained only by force. The British could not win precisely because the Americans were fighting a popular war.

Although an analogy with guerrilla warfare can give us some suggestion as to the extent of patriotism during the Revolution, we need more specific information. One fruitful technique for evaluating the loyalties of the inarticulate is to look at them under pressure—in prison. With little chance of exchange, amidst starvation and disease, and ruled over by cruel and corrupt administrators, captured American seamen were offered a way out: they could join the Royal Navy. Most remained patriots, and they were very self-conscious about it. Instead of defecting, they resisted, escaping, burning their prisons, and defiantly celebrating the Fourth of July. Separated from their captains and governing themselves for the first time, on their own they organized into disciplined groups with bylaws: in microcosm the prisoners went through the whole process of setting up a constitution. Men from all over the colonies discovered that they were Americans, that they had common grievances and a common enemy. Studies of other men in similar situations would give our generalizations about the role of the inarticulate in the American Revolution more substance than they presently have. . . .

The American Revolution can best be re-examined from a point of view which assumes that all men are created equal, and rational, and that since they can think and reason they can make their own history. These assumptions are nothing more nor less than the democratic credo. All of our history needs re-examination from this perspective. The history of the powerless, the inarticulate, the poor has not yet begun to be written because they have been treated no more fairly by historians than they have been treated by their contemporaries.

15

R. R. Palmer
"The most distinctive work of the Revolution was in finding a method"

At Princeton University since 1936, R. R. Palmer is one of the relatively few historians in this country who have worked extensively in the field of comparative history—in this case, the inter-relationships of revolutions in the Western world during the late eighteenth and early nineteenth centuries. The comparative study of revolutionary movements provides a breadth of view and a variety of perspectives that can sometimes reveal more than would isolated studies. Through his full knowledge of the history of Western Europe, too, Mr. Palmer is better able to understand the unique characteristics of the American Revolution.

If it be asked what the American Revolution distinctively contributed to the world's stock of ideas, the answer might go somewhat along these lines. It did not contribute primarily a social doctrine—for although a certain skepticism toward social rank was an old American attitude, and possibly even a gift to mankind, it long antedated the Revolution, which did not so much cut down, as prevent the growth of, an aristocracy

SOURCE. R. R. Palmer, *The Age of the Democratic Revolution: A Political History of Europe and America, 1760–1800: The Challenge, I.* Princeton, N. J.: Princeton University Press, 1959, pp. 213–15, 239–240, 240–41, 242, 253–54, 259–260, 282. Reprinted by permission of Princeton University Press.

of European type. It did not especially contribute economic ideas—for the Revolution had nothing to teach on the production or distribution of goods, and the most advanced parties objected to private wealth only when it became too closely associated with government. They aimed at a separation of economic and political spheres, by which men of wealth, while free to get rich, should not have a disproportionate influence on government, and, on the other hand, government and public emoluments should not be used as a means of livelihood for an otherwise impecunious and unproductive upper class.

The American Revolution was a political movement, concerned with liberty, and with power. Most of the ideas involved were by no means distinctively American. There was nothing peculiarly American in the concepts, purely as concepts, of natural liberty and equality. They were admitted by conservatives, and were taught in the theological faculty at the Sorbonne. Nor could Americans claim any exclusive understanding of the ideas of government by contract or consent, or the sovereignty of the people, or political representation, or the desirability of independence from foreign rule, or natural rights, or the difference between natural law and positive law, or between certain fundamental laws and ordinary legislation, or the separation of powers, or the federal union of separate states. All these ideas were perfectly familiar in Europe, and that is why the American Revolution was of such interest to Europeans.

THE DISTINCTIVENESS OF AMERICAN POLITICAL IDEAS

The most distinctive work of the Revolution was in finding a method, and furnishing a model, for putting these ideas into practical effect. It was in the implementation of similar ideas that Americans were more successful than Europeans. "In the last fifty years," wrote General Bonaparte to Citizen Talleyrand in 1797, "there is only one thing that I can see that we have really defined, and that is the sovereignty of the people. But we have had no more success in determining what is constitutional, than in allocating the different powers of government."

And he said more peremptorily, on becoming Emperor in 1804, that the time had come "to constitute the Nation." He added: "I am the constituent power."

The problem throughout much of America and Europe, for half a century, was to "constitute" new government, and in a measure new societies. The problem was to find a constituent power. Napoleon offered himself to Europe in this guise. The Americans solved the problem by the device of the constitutional convention, which, revolutionary in origin, soon became institutionalized in the public law of the United States.

The constitutional convention in theory embodied the sovereignty of the people. The people chose it for a specific purpose, not to govern, but to set up institutions of government. The convention, acting as the sovereign people, proceeded to draft a constitution and a declaration of rights. Certain "natural" or "inalienable" rights of the citizen were thus laid down at the same time as the powers of government. It was the constitution that created the powers of government, defined their scope, gave them legality, and balanced them one against another. The constitution was written and comprised in a single document. The constitution and accompanying declaration, drafted by the convention, must, in the developed theory, be ratified by the people. The convention thereupon disbanded and disappeared, lest its members have a vested interest in the offices they created. The constituent power went into abeyance, leaving the work of government to the authorities now constituted. The people, having exercised sovereignty, now came under government. Having made law, they came under law. They put themselves voluntarily under restraint. At the same time, they put restraint upon government. All government was limited government; all public authority must keep within the bounds of the constitution and of the declared rights. There were two levels of law, a higher law or constitution that only the people could make or amend, through constitutional conventions or bodies similarly empowered; and a statutory law, to be made and unmade, within the assigned limits, by legislators to whom the constitution gave this function.

Such was the theory, and it was a distinctively American one.

European thinkers, in all their discussion of a political or social contract, of government by consent and of sovereignty of the people, had not clearly imagined the people as actually contriving a constitution and creating the organs of government. They lacked the idea of the people as a constituent power. . . .

The first and greatest effect of the American Revolution in Europe was to make Europeans believe, or rather feel, often in a highly emotional way, that they lived in a rare era of momentous change. They saw a kind of drama of the continents. This was the generation that read Raynal's *Philosophical History of European Establishments in the Two Indies,* a huge work published in Paris in 1770, which went through fifty-five editions in five or six languages within thirty years. It was a long humanitarian recital of the evils brought upon the world by European greed and colonialism. Seen against this background, the successful War of American Independence presented itself as a great act of retribution on a cosmic stage. There were many Europeans who said that America would someday, in its turn, predominate over Europe. Nor was this the view of enthusiasts only. No reports were more coldly analytical than those sent home by the Venetian ambassadors. The Venetian Ambassador in Paris observed in 1783, in a report written in secrecy and with no intention to be pompous: "If only the union of the Provinces is preserved, it is reasonable to expect that, with the favorable effects of time, and of European arts and sciences, it will become the most formidable power in the world."

More than power was involved, and more than the grandiose conceptions of an embryonic geopolitics. The American Revolution coincided with the climax of the Age of Enlightenment. It was itself, in some degree, the product of this age. There were many in Europe, as there were in America, who saw in the American Revolution a lesson and an encouragement for mankind. It proved that the liberal ideas of the Enlightenment might be put into practice. It showed, or was assumed to show, that ideas of the rights of man and the social contract, of liberty and equality, of responsible citizenship and popular sovereignty, of religious freedom, freedom of thought and speech, separation of powers and deliberately contrived written constitutions, need not remain in the realm of speculation, among the writers of books, but could be made the actual fabric of public life among real people, in this world, now.

Thus was created an American myth, or mirage, or dream, "the first of those great movements of secular mysticism," to quote a recent author, "which modern man has been experimenting with for the last two hundred years." It was "essentially the belief that certain key doctrines were achieving their first realization in the United States." The first realization was not to be the last. Hence came an expectancy of change, a sense of great events already begun, a consciousness of a new era, a receptivity to that attempt at world renewal·soon to be made in France. And if anyone thinks that Americans had nothing to do with launching this *mystique* of world revolution, let him examine the Great Seal of the United States, conveniently printed on the back of the dollar bill, with its penetrating eye, its everlasting pyramid dated 1776, and its Latin motto: *Novus Ordo Saeclorum....*

There were great differences, country by country, in the way in which Europeans reacted [to the American Revolution]. At one extreme, there were three countries in which admirers of the American Revolution enjoyed, or seized, the opportunity for political action in their own affairs. These three were England, Ireland, and the United Provinces. In England those who most warmly sympathized with America were kept busy attending meetings, forming associations, drafting plans, and conducting propaganda for parliamentary reform. In Ireland and in the Dutch provinces they formed militia companies, wore uniforms, attended drills, and built up an actual revolutionary pressure which produced real results. As one of the Dutch leaders said, to follow the example of America meant that all should be ready, "every man with his musket." Where action of such positive kind was possible there was less need to vent one's feelings in poems, orations, pamphlets and treatises on distant lands.

At the other extreme, south of the Alps and Pyrenees, the American Revolution seems in these years to have produced little commotion. Carli's *Lettere americane* of 1780 proves to be about the Lost Atlantis. It was with Latin America that these countries had their contacts, and the important works of two American-born Jesuits, in refuge in Italy after the dissolution of the Jesuit order—Molina on Chile and Clavigero on Mexico—were written in Italy during the American Revolution, on which, however, they gave no information. Knowledge of British America had long been scarce in southern Europe, and the governments there had no desire for their subjects to learn about it now. Probably beneath the political censorship there were stirrings of interest that cannot now be traced. . . .

Between the two extremes, in the middle zone of France and Germany, there was a far more lively interest in the American Revolution than in the south, together with a more highly developed press and a wider penetration of the liberalism of the Enlightenment, while on the other hand there was no chance for private persons to do anything in the way of practical politics, as in Holland and the British Isles. The result was an incredible outburst of discussion, speculation, rhapsody, and argument, a veritable intoxication with the *rêve américain*. . . . Europeans were made conscious of the American Revolution in many ways, through the press, through discussions in reading clubs or Masonic lodges, through the reports of returned soldiers, and through the deliberate propaganda of Americans and others. All worked upon a basic receptivity in Europe, since the revolution in America gave the opportunity for discussion, in a colorful and dramatic context, of those general ideas about government and politics which had come to occupy the European mind. . . .

America was a screen on which Europe projected its own visions. Europe was divided and restless within itself, with both aristocratic and middle-class ways of life making increasing claims to recognition. It set value both on personal merit and on inherited family status. A growing demand for equality went along with a more troubled class consciousness; and a belief that affairs should be conducted by an elite, either of bureaucratic officials or of constituted bodies that had become largely hereditary, conflicted with a vague and widespread desire, among people hitherto outside the political scene, to take part in affairs, to do good for society, to play the patriot, to act the citizen. Views of America were of every kind, from the enthusiastic to the disgusted, from the revolutionary to the conservative, from the mystical and the moralizing to the sharply political, and from the highly unreal to the concretely realistic. . . .

That America was the hope of humanity, the asylum of liberty, the beacon for all ages to come, was the common talk among the more fervid in France. The Swiss Iselin apparently agreed with a letter that he published in his journal, to the effect that anyone favoring oppression of the Americans sinned against mankind. In Germany when Schlözer criticized the Americans as rebels he was answered by Jakob Mauvillon, who, defending the principle of the sovereignty of the people, found "a secret bond . . . which links the cause of the Colonies with the welfare and uplifting of the human race." The Italian, Castiglioni, who was not actually much impressed by what he saw across the Atlantic, allowed nevertheless that in time the American Revolution would have momentous consequences for Europe. It would be tedious to repeat examples.

There were many who stood apart from, and even opposed, the idealization of America, nor did they include only those who, like Schlözer and the other Hanoverians, more or less deliberately publicized a British view. In Germany the warmest enthusiasts for America were generally unknown and obscure people. There was an unformulated popular sentiment in favor of America. There was in some circles a literary republicanism, but in others there was a conservatism that already used conservative language. Thus Wekhrlin, who along with Schlözer was one of the founders of modern German journalism, thought of the Americans as a rabble in arms, ridiculed those in Germany who "only learned about men in a dream world or in Masonic lodges," and held that "the great words Freedom, Constitution, Country, turn the head of some people." The professional men of learning, who already heavily predominated in the expression of German opinion, tended to disapprove of rebellion, or at the most to preserve a kind of neutrality,

to avoid discussion of the rights of the question, to give factual
narratives of events in America, and to maintain a scholarly
view by publishing the arguments and the documents from
both British and American sources. . . .

In France the war against England, by making zeal for
America coincide with French patriotism, removed the restraints both of conservatism and of mere objective study.
Where many Germans saw the American war simply as an
important dispute, the French saw it as a crusade. Yet even
in France there were doubters. Linguet, a kind of anti-*phi-
losophe,* attributed the American Revolution to an overdose
of eighteenth-century philosophy. This was in 1777, long before
Burke and others offered the same explanation of the revolution
in France. Another laughed at pro-American myth-makers—
those "orators, poets, panegyrists of romantic virtues and legislators of societies that will never exist." Some who did in fact
strongly sympathize with the Americans tried nevertheless to
combat, as did Jefferson himself, the more absurd ideas that
were current in France. One of these was the Marquis de
Chastellux, who had been a major-general in Rochambeau's
army, and who, having written a little tract *De la félicité pub-
lique,* was no enemy of the human race.

But in France, unlike Germany, the American Dream could
not be kept down. There were too many who preferred dreams
to reality. Brissot affords an excellent example. The French
Revolution was to make him famous; he was to be the virtual
head of the French government in 1792, and the man who more
than anyone else took France into war with Europe. Before
1789 he was one of the not very numerous people in France
who were already true revolutionaries. He was outraged at
Chastellux' attempt to moderate the excitement over America.
"Cruel man! Even if it were an illusion would you still dissipate
it? It would be dear to us, it would be useful in consoling
the man of virtue. . . ."

The effects [in Europe] of the American Revolution, as a
revolution, were imponderable but very great. It inspired the
sense of a new era. It added a new content to the conception
of progress. It gave a whole new dimension to ideas of liberty

and equality made familiar by the Enlightenment. It got people into the habit of thinking more concretely about political questions, and made them more readily critical of their own governments and society. It dethroned England, and set up America, as a model for those seeking a better world. It brought written constitutions, declarations of rights, and constituent conventions into the realm of the possible. The apparition on the other side of the Atlantic of certain ideas already familiar in Europe made such ideas seem more truly universal, and confirmed the habit of thinking in terms of humanity at large. Whether fantastically idealized or seen in a factual way, whether as mirage or as reality, America made Europe seem unsatisfactory to many people of the middle and lower classes, and to those of the upper classes who wished them well. It made a good many Europeans feel sorry for themselves, and induced a kind of spiritual flight from the Old Regime.

16

Hannah Arendt
"It is as though the American Revolution was achieved in a kind of ivory tower"

Hannah Arendt, a political scientist and author, was born in Hanover, Germany, and spent some thirty-five years in various parts of Europe before coming to the United States. In this country she was successively a social worker, editor, and on the faculties of various American universities before going to the New School for Social Research in New York.

This varied and international background is no doubt partly responsible for the broad, interpretative approach that appears in On Revolution *(1963), from which the following is reprinted. Although the comparative approach is similar to that of R. R. Palmer, the conclusions are quite different.*

The superior wisdom of the American founders in theory and practice is conspicuous and impressive enough, and yet has never carried with it sufficient persuasiveness and plausibility to prevail in the tradition of revolution. It is as though the American Revolution was achieved in a kind of ivory tower into which the fearful spectacle of huamn misery, the haunting

SOURCE. Hannah Arendt, *On Revolution*. New York: The Viking Press, 1963, pp. 90-91, 217-220. Copyright© 1963 by Hannah Arendt. All rights reserved. Reprinted by permission of the Viking Press, Inc.

voices of abject poverty, never penetrated. And this was, and remained for a long time, the spectacle and the voice not of humanity but of human-kind. Since there were no sufferings around them that could have aroused their passions, no over-whelmingly urgent needs that would have tempted them to submit to necessity, no pity to lead them astray from reason, the men of the American Revolution remained men of action from beginning to end, from the Declaration of Independence to the framing of the Constitution. Their sound realism was never exposed to the absurd hope that man, whom Christianity had held to be sinful and corrupt in his nature, might still be revealed to be an angel. Since passion had never tempted them in its noblest form as compassion, they found it easy to think of passion in terms of desire and to banish from it any connota-tion of its original meaning, which is παβείγ, to suffer *and* to endure. This lack of experience gives their theories, even if they are sound, an air of lightheartedness, a certain weightless-ness, which may well put into jeopardy their durability. For, humanly speaking, it is endurance which enables man to create durability and continuity. Their thought did not carry them any further than to the point of understanding government in the image of individual reason and construing the rule of government over the governed according to the age-old model of the rule of reason over the passions. To bring the "irration-ality" of desires and emotions under the control of rationality was, of course, a thought dear to the Enlightenment, and as such was quickly found wanting in many respects, especially in its facile and superficial equation of thought with reason and of reason with rationality....

If there was a single event that shattered the bonds between the New World and the countries of the old Continent, it was the French Revolution, which, in the view of its contemporaries, might never have come to pass without the glorious example on the other side of the Atlantic. It was not the fact of revolution but its disastrous course and the collapse of the French republic which eventually led to the severance of the strong spiritual and political ties between America and Europe that had prevailed all through the seventeenth and eighteenth centuries. Thus,

Condorcet's *Influence de la Révolution d'Amérique sur l'Europe,* published three years before the storming of the Bastille, was to mark, temporarily at least, the end and not the beginning of an Atlantic civilization. One is tempted to hope that the rift which occurred at the end of the eighteenth century is about to heal in the middle of the twentieth century, when it has become rather obvious that Western civilization has its last chance of survival in an Atlantic community; and among the signs to justify this hope is perhaps also the fact that since the Second World War historians have been more inclined to consider the Western world as a whole than they have been since the early nineteenth century.

Whatever the future may hold in store for us, the estrangement of the two continents after the eighteenth-century revolutions has remained a fact of great consequence. It was chiefly during this time that the New World lost its political significance in the eyes of the leading strata in Europe, that America ceased to be the land of the free and became almost exclusively the promised land of the poor. To be sure, the attitude of Europe's upper classes toward the alleged materialism and vulgarity of the New World was an almost automatic outgrowth of the social and cultural snobbism of the rising middle classes, and as such of no great importance. What mattered was that the European revolutionary tradition in the nineteenth century did not show more than a passing interest in the American Revolution or in the development of the American republic. In conspicuous contrast to the eighteenth century, when the political thought of the *philosophes,* long before the outbreak of an American Revolution, was attuned to events and institutions in the New World, revolutionary political thought in the nineteenth and twentieth centuries has proceeded as though there never had occurred a revolution in the New World and as though there never had been any American notions and experiences in the realm of politics and government worth thinking about.

In recent times, when revolution has become one of the most common occurrences in the political life of nearly all countries and continents, the failure to incorporate the American Revolution into the revolutionary tradition has boomeranged upon the foreign policy of the United States, which begins to pay an exorbitant price for world-wide ignorance and for native oblivion. The point is unpleasantly driven home when even revolutions on the American continent speak and act as though they knew by heart the texts of revolutions in France, in Russia, and in China, but had never heard of such a thing as an American Revolution. Less spectacular perhaps, but certainly no less real, are the consequences of the American counterpart to the world's ignorance, her own failure to remember that a revolution gave birth to the United States and that the republic was brought into existence by no "historical necessity" and no organic development, but by a deliberate act: the foundation of freedom. Failure to remember is largely responsible for the intense fear of revolution in this country, for it is precisely this fear that attests to the world at large how right they are to think of revolution only in terms of the French Revolution. Fear of revolution has been the hidden *leitmotif* of postwar American foreign policy in its desperate attempts at stabilization of the status quo, with the result that American power and prestige were used and misused to support obsolete and corrupt political regimes that long since had become objects of hatred and contempt among their own citizens.

Failure to remember and, with it, failure to understand have been conspicuous whenever, in rare moments, the hostile dialogue with Soviet Russia touched upon matters of principle. When we were told that by freedom we understood free enterprise, we did very little to dispel this monstrous falsehood, and all too often we have acted as though we too believed that it was wealth and abundance which were at stake in the postwar conflict between the "revolutionary" countries in the East and the West. Wealth and economic well-being, we have asserted, are the fruits of freedom, while we should have been the first to know that this kind of "happiness" was the blessing of this country prior to the Revolution, and that its cause was natural abundance under "mild government," and neither political freedom nor the unchained, unbridled "private initiative" of capitalism, which in the absence of natural wealth has led everywhere to unhappiness and mass poverty. Free enterprise, in other words, has been an unmixed blessing only in this country, and it is a minor blessing compared with the truly political freedoms, such as freedom of speech and thought, of assembly and association, even under the best conditions. Economic growth may one day turn out to be a curse rather than a good, and under no conditions can it either lead into freedom or constitute a proof for its existence. A competition between America and Russia, therefore, with regard to production and standards of living, trips to the moon and scientific discoveries, may be very interesting in many respects; its outcome may even be understood as a demonstration of the stamina and gifts of the two nations involved, as well as of the value of their different social manners and customs. There is only one question this outcome, whatever it may be, will never be able to decide, and that is which form of government is better, a tyranny or a free republic. Hence, in terms of the American Revolution, the response to the Communist bid to equal and surpass the Western countries in production of consumer goods and economic growth should have been to rejoice over the new good prospects opening up to the people of the Soviet Union and its satellites, to be relieved that at least the conquest of poverty on a world-wide scale could constitute an issue of common concern, and then to remind our opponents that serious conflicts would not rise out of the disparity between two economic systems but only out of the conflict between freedom and tyranny, between the institutions of liberty, born out of the triumphant victory of a revolution, and the various forms of domination (from Lenin's one-party dictatorship to Stalin's totalitarianism to Khrushchev's attempts at an enlightened despotism) which came in the aftermath of a revolutionary defeat.

SUGGESTIONS FOR ADDITIONAL READING

An immense literature exists on the causes, character, and consequences of the American Revolution. From this it is possible to choose works that are most important to an understanding of the Revolution and by which, at the same time, one can follow the changing interpretations of the last two centuries.

Six recent works deal with the historiography of the Revolution: Edmund S. Morgan, *The American Revolution: A Review of Changing Interpretations* (1958); Merrill Jensen, "Historians and the Nature of the American Revolution," in *The Reinterpretation of Early American History: Essays in Honor of John Edwin Pomfret*, Ray Allen Billington, ed. (1966), pp. 101–27; Jack P. Greene, "The Flight from Determinism: A Review of Recent Literature on the Coming of the American Revolution," *South Atlantic Quarterly*, **61** (1962), 235–59; Page Smith, "David Ramsay and the Causes of the American Revolution," *William and Mary Quarterly*, 3d sev., **17** (1960), 51–77; Wesley Frank Craven, "The Revolutionary Era," in *The Reconstruction of American History*, John Higham, ed. (1962), pp. 46–63; and Richard B. Morris, *The American Revolution Reconsidered* (1968). Each of these reveals, incidentally or deliberately, much of its author's own interpretation.

Among the more important works by patriot historians are David Ramsay, *History of the American Revolution* (2 vols., 1789); Mercy Otis Warren, *Rise, Progress and Termination of the American Revolution* (3 vols., 1805); and the Reverend William Gordon, *The History of the Rise, Progress, and Establishment, of the Independence of the United States of America* (4 vols., 1788). Useful histories by loyalists include George Chalmers, *An Introduction to the History of the Revolt of the American Colonies* (2 vols., 1845); Joseph Galloway, *Historical and Political Reflections on the Rise and Progress of the American Rebellion* (1780); Thomas Hutchinson, *The History of the Colony and*

Province of Massachusetts-Bay, Lawrence S. Mayo, ed. (3 vols., 1936) ; Thomas Jones, *History of New York during the Revolutionary War* (1879); and *Peter Oliver's Origin & Progress of the American Rebellion*, Douglas Adair and John A. Schutz, eds. (1961).

Bancroft's interpretation is best read in "The Author's Last Revision" of his *History of the United States of America, from the Discovery of the Continent* (6 vols., 1883–1885). The Whig interpretation continued long after Bancroft and exists, though greatly modified, in such works as Claude Van Tyne, *The Causes of the War of Independence* (1922), and John C. Miller, *Origins of the American Revolution* (1945), not to mention the writings of the neo-Whig historians.

Of the revisionist studies that appeared early in the twentieth century to emphasize the importance of social and economic factors, four were to have an immense influence: Carl Becker, *The History of Political Parties in the Province of New York, 1760–1776* (1909) ; Charles A. Beard, *An Economic Interpretation of the Constitution of the United States* (1913) ; Arthur M. Schlesinger, *The Colonial Merchants and the American Revolution, 1763–1776* (1918) ; and J. Franklin Jameson, *The American Revolution Considered as a Social Movement* (1926). Anyone wishing to follow this approach through the years might find the following useful: Allen Nevins, *The American States during and after the Revolution* (1924) ; E. B. Greene, *The Revolutionary Generation, 1763–1790* (1943) ; Merrill Jensen, *The Articles of Confederation* (1940), *The New Nation* (1950), and *The Founding of a Nation: A History of the American Revolution, 1763–1776* (1968) ; Elisha P. Douglass, *Rebels and Democrats* (1955) ; and Jackson Turner Main, "Government by the People: The American Revolution and the Democratization of the Legislatures," *William and Mary Quarterly*, 3d ser., **23** (1966), 341–407. For propaganda during the Revolution see Philip Davidson, *Propaganda and the American Revolution, 1763–1783* (1941), and Arthur M. Schlesinger, *Prelude to Independence: the Newspaper War on Britain, 1764–1776* (1958).

Among the more important works by imperial historians that directly or indirectly reveal their interpretation of the American Revolution are three volumes by George Louis Beer, *British Colonial Policy, 1754–1765* (1907); *The Origins of the British Colonial System, 1578–1660* (1908); and *The Old Colonial System, 1660–1754* (1912) ; Sydney G. Fisher, *The Struggle for American Independence* (1908) ; Charles M. Andrews, *The Colonial Background of the American Revolution* (1924), and *The Colonial Period of American History* (4 vols., 1934–1938), especially Volume 4; Leonard Woods Labaree, *Royal Government in America* (1930); and Lawrence Henry Gipson, *The British Empire before the*

American Revolution (13 vols., 1936–1967). Gipson's interpretation appears more concisely in *The Coming of the Revolution, 1763–1775* (1954).

In addition to many state and local studies of the loyalists, there are some general works. Early was Claude H. Van Tyne, *The Loyalists in the American Revolution* (1902), whereas more recent are William H. Nelson, *The American Tory* (1961) and Wallace Brown, *The King's Friends: the Composition and Motives of the American Loyalist Claimants* (1966). The British failure to use loyalist strength in America is the subject of Paul H. Smith, *Loyalists and Redcoats: A Study in British Revolutionary Policy* (1964).

The characteristics of the neo-Whig interpretation appear, in varying degrees and with differing emphases, in Edmund S. Morgan, *The Birth of the Republic, 1763–1789* (1956), and Edmund S. Morgan and Helen M. Morgan, *The Stamp Act Crisis; Prologue to Revolution* (1953); Daniel Boorstin, *The Genius of American Politics* (1953); Louis Hartz, *The Liberal Tradition in America* (1955); Robert E. Brown, *Middle-Class Democracy and the Revolution in Massachusetts, 1691–1780* (1955); Cecelia M. Kenyon, "Republicanism and Radicalism in the American Revolution: An Old-Fashioned Interpretation," *William and Mary Quarterly,* **19** (1962), 153–82; O. M. Dickerson, *The Navigation Acts and the American Revolution* (1951); and Bernhard Knollenberg, *Origin of the American Revolution, 1759–1766* (1960). For criticisms or modifications of the neo-Whig approach see William H. Nelson, "The Revolutionary Character of the American Revolution," *American Historical Review,* **70** (1965), 998–1014; Richard B. Morris, *The American Revolution Reconsidered* (1967); and the essays by Gordon S. Wood and Merrill Jensen reprinted in this book.

For the intellectual origins of the American Revolution a classic work remains Moses Coit Tyler, *The Literary History of the American Revolution, 1763–1783* (2 vols., 1897). Some of the British background is provided in Caroline Robbins, *The Eighteenth Century Commonwealthman* (1959), and three works perform a similar role for the American colonies: Max Savelle, *Seeds of Liberty* (1948); Clinton Rossiter, *Seedtime of the Republic* (1953); and Daniel J. Boorstin, *The Americans: The Colonial Experience* (1958). A comparative study is J. R. Pole, *Political Representation in England and the Origins of the American Republic* (1966). More directly related to the Revolution are Carl Becker, *The Declaration of Independence* (1922); E. Trevor Colbourn, *The Lamp of Experience: Whig History and the Intellectual Origins of the American Revolution* (1965); and Bernard Bailyn, *The Ideological Origins of the American Revolution* (1967). For the religious background of the Revolution see Perry Miller, "From the Covenant to the Revival," in James Ward Smith and A. Leland Jamison, eds., *The Shaping of American Religion*, 1 (1961), 322–68; Carl Bridenbaugh, *Mitre and Sceptre* (1962); and Alan Heimert, *Religion and the American Mind: from the Great Awakening to the Revolution* (1966).

There are, of course, many studies which, although sympathetic to one or another of the various interpretations of the American Revolution, are of interest primarily for their treatment of special aspects of that subject. One might include in this category Samuel F. Bemis, *The Diplomacy of the American Revolution* (1935); Richard W. Van Alstyne, *Empire and Independence: The International History of the American Revolution* (1965); Carl Bridenbaugh, *Cities in Revolt* (1955); John R. Alden, *The South in the Revolution*, 1763–1789 (1957); Carl Ubbelohde, *The Vice-Admiralty Courts and the American Revolution* (1960); Jesse Lemisch, "Jack Tar in the Streets: Merchant Seamen in the Politics of Revolutionary America," *William and Mary Quarterly*, 3d ser., 25 (1968), 371–407; Jack P. Greene, *The Quest for Power; The Lower Houses of Assembly in the Southern Royal Colonies*, 1689–1776 (1963); Benjamin Quarles, *The Negro in the American Revolution* (1961); and Benjamin Woods Labaree, *The Boston Tea Party* (1964).

The violent Western uprisings that complicated the revolutionary movement are the subject of Brooke Hindle, "The March of the Paxton Boys," *William and Mary Quarterly*, 3d ser., 3 (1946), 461–82; John S. Bassett, "The Regulators of North Carolina (1765–1771)," American Historical Association, *Annual Report* (1894), pp. 141–212; *The Carolina Backcountry on the Eve of the Revolution: The Journal and Other Writings of Charles Woodmason, Anglican Itinerant*, Richard J. Hooker, ed. (1953); and Richard M. Brown, *The South Carolina Regulators* (1963).

For the thought and behavior of those in power in England one may consult Sir Lewis Namier, *The Structure of Politics at the Accession of George III* (1929), *England in the Age of the American Revolution* (1930), and Bernard Donoughue, *British Politics and the American Revolution: the Path to War*, 1773–1775 (1964). Many of the Namierist findings are condensed in Eric Robson, *The American Revolution in Its Political and Military Aspects*, 1763–1783 (1955).

General accounts of the war years are John C. Miller, *The Triumph of Freedom*, 1775–1783 (1948), and John Richard Alden, *The American Revolution*, 1775–1783 (1954). A useful historiographical study is Don Higginbotham, "American Historians and the Military History of the American Revolution," *American Historical Review*, 70 (1964), 18–34.

The lively controversy over the validity of the Beard-Jensen thesis of democratic revolution and conservative counter-revolution can be traced in the following: Cecelia M. Kenyon, "Men of Little Faith: The Anti-Federalists on the Nature of Representative Government," *William and Mary Quarterly,* 3d ser., **12** (1955), 3–43; Robert E. Brown, *Charles Beard and the Constitution* (1956); Forrest McDonald, *We the People: the Economic Origins of the Constitution* (1958); Lee Benson, *Turner and Beard; American Historical Writing Reconsidered* (1960); Jackson T. Main, *The Antifederalists; Critics of the Constitution,* 1781–1788 (1961); and Staughton Lynd, *Class Conflict, Slavery, and the United States Constitution* (1968).

Some scholars have attempted to assess the impact of the American Revolution on other parts of the world. For its influence in Europe see R. R. Palmer, *The Age of the Democratic Revolution* (2 vols., 1959, 1964), and Hannah Arendt, *On Revolution* (1963). For the Revolution's influence on the modern Asian and African revolutions see Carl N. Degler, "The American Past: An Unsuspected Obstacle in Foreign Affairs," *American Scholar,* **32** (1963), 192–209, and Seymour Martin Lipset, *The First New Nation: The United States in Historical and Comparative Perspective* (1963). The influences on Canada appear in Gustave Lanctot, *Canada and the American Revolution* (1967). A comparison of the American with subsequent revolutions is R. R. Palmer, "The Revolution," in *The Comparative Approach to American History,* C. Vann Woodward, ed. (1968), pp. 47–61.